THE MAKER'S ATELIER

The Essential Collection

THE MAKER'S ATELIER

The Essential Collection

Sewing with Style

Frances Tobin

Photography by Amelia Shepherd
and Katya De Grunwald

quadrille

Contents

Hello, and welcome to The Maker's Atelier Essential Collection

My name is Frances Tobin and I started The Maker's Atelier to publish my own dressmaking patterns. My background is in the fashion industry where I worked as a designer, but wherever I've worked and whatever clothes have been available to me, I have always preferred to make my own. The whole making process fascinates me and has done since I was a child.

Looking back, I was so lucky; I come from a large family with brothers and sisters – all with their own sense of style – and a mother who was quite happy to let us experiment. Every time she took me clothes shopping we could never find anything that I wanted to wear. The clothes available to young girls did not look like the clothes I was seeing in my older sisters' fashion magazines. The cut, the colour or the feel of the fabric were wrong; at the age of six I aspired to look like Jean Shrimpton. So my mother would end up making my clothes, allowing me to choose the fabric and style. She would get me to watch as she cut out and made my clothes, and that is how I learnt to sew.

By the time I was in my teens I would spend all week at school dreaming about what I was going to wear on Saturday night. I was constantly changing my image so I would usually have to make or reinvent something. I had to be quite creative as there was always a lack of time and money. I'd see what I could requisition at home, or scour the local charity shops for fabric or clothes that I could cut up and remake.

It was inevitable that I would become a fashion designer; I had little interest in anything else. My first degree was in fashion textile design where I specialised in knitwear. I learnt about fibres and yarns, dyestuffs and colour, fabric construction and garment design. This led to an MA at The Royal College of Art and a career in fashion.

I love fashion, it is constantly changing, reinventing and challenging what we see as desirable; but beyond fashion, I love style. Style is different from fashion; fashion is of the moment, whereas style is a way of doing things. It is how you put your look together. It doesn't have to be extraordinary or challenging, it's what feels right to you. I have developed my own style through my dressmaking. Through the process of choosing fabric and deciding what to make, I have learnt what suits me. I have found I do not like very fitted clothes – they do not flatter me and I find them too restrictive. I like to be able to move freely in a fluid shape that skims the body. I like to keep things simple and uncluttered, and then layer on a few accessories.

Like most people who sew, I love finding beautiful materials and spend hours in fabric shops looking for inspiration for what to make. One fateful day I was in my local fabric shop, Ditto, when Gill Thornley, the owner, suggested I publish my own patterns. Though I haven't used shop-bought patterns for years – they just don't have the look I want – I was sceptical of this idea at first. But then I realised that here was an opportunity to create something special. I wanted to bring back the excitement I'd felt as a child watching my mother and older sisters discuss the latest styles in the Vogue designer pattern range. Those styles were far more fashionable than the clothes available in the shops of our provincial high street.

So the idea for The Maker's Atelier came about. I would take the key shapes from current fashion trends, refine them into wearable styles, and translate them into clear dressmaking patterns. A range of patterns that was desirable, wearable and make-able.

The Maker's Atelier isn't for everyone; it has a distinctive style, but one that resonates with women of all sizes and ages. Women who know how to dress well but can't always find what they want in the shops. It is a style that has evolved through my years of making clothes and working as a fashion designer. I have found that it is my simpler, more pared-back styles that are the most successful; I like the fabric and the cut to do the work, rather than fancy detail.

The Essential Collection is an extension of The Maker's Atelier. For this collection I have taken the styles that I have found indispensable over the years and refined them further to create a range of versatile separates made up of three tops and three bottoms, with a piece of outwear and a really useful accessory. The clean lines and simple shapes mean that each garment works beautifully in a variety of fabrics and will flatter a broad range of sizes.

Each piece in the collection has been given its own chapter in the book; you will learn how the shape evolved and I offer suggestions for how it can be worn. Illustrated, step-by-step instructions are given for how to make the garment in one form, followed by a section on how to vary this to create two or three very different garments; not only through using different fabrics, but also by changing elements or details of construction. The patterns are in a full range of sizes (see page 14 for more on sizing), and can be found in the envelope at the back of the book.

I hope that you will be inspired by *The Essential Collection* to not only make what you see here, but also to develop your own ideas, in the fabrics you like, creating a collection that's unique to you and your style.

Frances

Choosing and using fabrics

One of the most exciting parts in the dressmaking process is finding your fabric. I spend hours looking at fabrics, checking the 'handle' to see how they drape and move. I can't separate fabric from clothes: when I see a fabric, it inspires what I want to make, and when I get an idea for a garment I know the sort of fabric I will need to make it. Fabric is an endless source of inspiration.

I find fabrics and trimmings all over the place, from fabric shops to flea markets and thrift shops. When I see something I really like, I'll buy three metres, even if I'm not sure what I'll use it for immediately. I know I'll regret not buying it. I never stop experimenting with new fabrics that I come across; I like to see what happens, some times with disastrous results, but I always learn something and broaden my sewing skills. When I'm working with a new fabric, I try out the stitch I'm thinking of using on offcuts of my fabric to perfect the finish before starting on my actual garment.

In *The Essential Collection* I have used a variety of fabrics. The pared-back style of the designs mean that the garments can be made in more than one fabric type. For every project there is a definitive garment, followed by variations created in different fabrics. Each fabric has a different effect on how the garment looks and can be worn. I hope you'll be inspired to be adventurous with your fabric selection, but still work with what feels right for you.

Choosing fabric can be overwhelming, there's often too much choice. When I can't decide, I ask for small samples that I take away so I have time to think, even if it's just while I have a cup of coffee. Try not to buy on price alone; some of my 'bargains' have never been used.

Here is a brief overview of the types of fabric I have used in this book, and some tips on working with them.

Woven fabric

Basic woven fabric is constructed with threads interwoven at right angles to each other. The threads running the length of the fabric are called the warp and the threads that run across the width are called the weft. This construction usually creates a fabric that is non-stretch in the warp or weft direction, although flexible on the bias – the angle of 45 degrees to warp or weft. Terms such as denim, canvas or twill, refer to the type of weave pattern.

There are also stretch woven fabrics where elastomeric yarn (such as Lycra) is included in the weave construction. These fabrics can stretch in one or both directions, depending on how the stretch yarn is added in the weaving process.

The other form of stretch woven is called a mechanical stretch. This is when a chemical finish is applied to the flat fabric causing it to shrink, and so creating a stretch when pulled. This stretch quality is not as strong or long-lasting as the stretch in a fabric with elastomeric yarn woven in to it, and

will not keep bouncing back. For example, if a tight-fitting skirt is made in a mechanical stretch fabric, it will 'seat' (the area around your bottom will become baggy) and not bounce back until it is washed again.

To sew with woven fabrics is fairly straightforward. Use a universal needle and straight stitch setting on your sewing machine. Vary the size of needle and stitch length to suit the fabric weight.

Knitted or jersey fabric

Knitted fabric is more complex in construction than woven fabric. In its most basic form it is made from a series of interlocking loops formed by a single thread looping through the last row of loops created. The resulting fabric is much more flexible than a woven fabric and can stretch in any direction.

In a similar way to mechanical stretch woven fabrics, if there is no elastomeric content in the yarn used, tight-fitting garments will 'seat'. T-shirts are often made from basic jersey with no added stretch, whereas the fabric used to make leggings will usually contain 4–6% stretch fibres, and performance sportswear and swimwear require a high percentage, approximately 18%.

Terms such as single or double jersey refer to the looped construction created by the needle bed set-up of the knitting machine. Single jersey is knitted on one bed, either flat or circular, so the loops always fall to the same side, creating a right and wrong side. Double jersey is knitted on a twin-bed set-up so there are usually two right, though sometimes differing, sides to the fabric; it is generally thicker and more stable to work with than single jersey.

To sew with knitted fabrics, use a ballpoint or jersey needle, which are designed to push the threads aside as they stitch. This prevents any laddering resulting from broken stitches.

Selecting the best sewing stitch for jersey fabrics is dependent on the amount of stretch required. Too little stretch and the sewing thread can break when the seam is stretched. For most side seams I like to use a plain straight stitch, but I apply a little tension to the fabric as I feed it under the machine foot. For waistbands and hems I use a zigzag stitch to allow for more stretch.

If my jersey fabric splays out, I generally use a steam iron, without pressing the fabric, to relax the fabric back into shape. In The Stretch Pencil Skirt there are a number of alternatives given for tackling hems in different ways (see page 29).

Technical fabrics

This is a term that refers to either woven or knitted fabrics that are coated or bonded with a chemically produced fabrication. PU and PVC are terms used for imitation leathers: PVC is a coated woven fabric with a high sheen like patent leather, and PU is a coated jersey fabric with a sheen finish and stretch qualities. Neoprene or scuba fabrics are bonded imitation rubber-like fabrics with a jersey backing for increased flexibility.

For technical fabrics with a jersey backing, I've found I get the best results from using a ballpoint or jersey needle. For woven-backed technical fabrics I use a universal needle, but if that has difficulty puncturing the fabric, I use a leather needle. I also lengthen the stitch length to get a smoother result.

The shiny surface of these fabrics can stick against the presser foot or machine plate. To avoid this, use a Teflon foot and make a template of non-stick baking parchment and secure it over the machine plate with tape.

For some PVC fabrics it can be impossible to pin seams in place before stitching, so try using a double-sided basting tape, or hold the pieces together with small bulldog or paper clips.

Keep technical fabrics rolled rather than folded to avoid permanent creasing.

Fine silky fabrics

I find these the trickiest fabrics to work with, but sometimes I can't resist them because of the luxurious, delicate handle.

Always use a fine needle, whether it's a universal or ballpoint needle. You can also get specialist needles for microfibre that I have used on natural silks as well as synthetic silky fabrics.

For buttonholes, try using a stick-on fabric stabiliser as used by embroiderers; I use Stitch and Tear. This will stop the fabric puckering up as you stitch.

Leather

I have used leather for versions of the original Raw-edge Coat (see page 106) and The Book Bag (see page 92).

When sewing with leather, select skins that are reasonably lightweight and flexible. If you have never sewn with suede or leather but would like to have a go, most suppliers have offcuts or part-skins at reduced prices, so you can try stitching before investing in the materials for a whole garment.

Leather has a tendency to tear at the seams if there are too many stitch perforations. To avoid this, increase the stitch length and always use a leather needle; its spear-like point cleanly cuts the stitch hole. Try out the strength of the proposed seam on an offcut.

As with technical fabrics (see above), it can be impossible to pin leather seams before stitching, so try using a double-sided basting tape, or hold the pieces together with small bulldog or paper clips. As with technical fabrics, keep leather or suede rolled, not folded.

Preparing fabric

Check the washing instructions for fabric when you buy it. If the fabric is washable, then wash it before cutting and making. The reason for doing this is that during the manufacturing process, fabrics are often 'stentered': that is, they are pulled into a uniform width and length and a finishing chemical is applied. The problem with this is that when the fabric is subsequently washed, it 'relaxes' back, or shrinks. So by pre-washing it before making it up, you can make sure that the garment you sew doesn't shrink.

If washing information isn't available, buy extra fabric to do a wash test. To do a wash test, cut a square 20 x 20cm (8 x 8in) and wash it at 40°C. Then, when it's washed and dried, re-measure it to check shrinkage and to review the handle of the fabric. If you don't like the result, make sure you only dry-clean the garment you are going to make.

Before washing lengths of fabric, unfold them and iron out any creases. Loosely load the fabric into your machine and use a liquid detergent. These steps should avoid any unevenness in colour fading, especially with indigo and pigment-dyed denim, or coloured linens.

Do not wash suede, leather or PVC, though I have washed PU – not because it would shrink but because it can have an unpleasant chemical smell.

Measuring, making a toile and fitting a garment

One of the benefits of making your own clothes is being able to get a fit that suits you. Very few people are a perfect match to a universal size chart, so here are some guidelines to help you get a great fit.

It is important to measure yourself accurately and then compare those measurements against the size chart given for each garment.

Bust: Measure the fullest part making sure the tape is level front and back.

Waist: Measure the narrowest part, just above the navel.

Hips: Measure the fullest part, usually at the top of the legs not at the top of the hipbone.

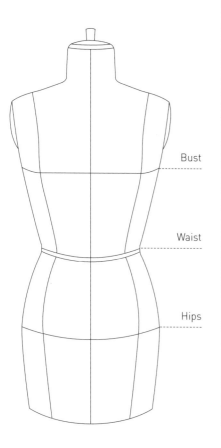

The size range for the patterns in *The Essential Collection* is from an 81cm (32in) bust up to a 116cm (46in) bust, spread over eight sizes for fitted patterns and four sizes for the looser styles. The measurements given in the sizing chart for each garment are the finished measurements of that garment and so include any ease that has been designed as part of the style: the majority of the styles are designed to be relaxed and comfortable to wear. The body measurements the garments are designed for are given in the charts on the page opposite.

The samples modelled in the book are all made in Size 3 for fitted garments and Size 3/4 for relaxed-fit garments. The women wearing them have varying body shapes, so you can see how the garments will fit and suit different figures and ages.

If your measurements fall between the sizes given, you can mark the variation on the paper pattern before cutting it out. For example, if your waist measurement is for a Size 3, but your hip measurement is a Size 4, then you can carefully draw in a personal pattern line graduating from one size to the other at the appropriate points. If you are slightly larger than the biggest size or smaller than the smallest size in the measurements chart, it is possible to grade the pattern up or down a little, but you should only attempt this if you are an experienced dressmaker.

Whether you have made adjustments or not, it is a good idea to make a toile (also known as a muslin). This is a practice garment made in inexpensive fabric to test a pattern out. For a very basic toile it is possible to purchase calico or unbleached cotton jersey for a fraction of the price of quality fabric. Make a simplified version of the garment, omitting details such as facings and hems. Then try on and alter the toile as necessary until it fits. Copy these amendments onto the original pattern or some plain pattern paper to make a personal version of the pattern.

Alternatively you could make a 'wearable toile'. This is the garment made up fully, but in an inexpensive fabric. It is a great way to practise the techniques required for that style and check for any sizing issues, and you will have a garment that at worst you can wear around the house or while gardening.

All fabrics respond differently, so throughout the making process, try on the garment inside out and check how it's fitting. This way you can mark any further alterations you wish to make – either with tailor's chalk or by pinning – and adjust accordingly. Remember to keep a note of any adjustments for when you want to make the same style again.

Bust

Waist

Hips

Fitted garments

The Stretch Pencil Skirt (see page 16), The Cigarette Pants (see page 46), and The Wrap Skirt (see page 112) patterns are in these eight sizes.

Size	1	2	3	4	5	6	7	8
Centimetres								
Bust	81	86	91	96	101	106	111	116
Waist	64	69	74	79	84	89	94	99
Hips	89	94	99	104	109	114	119	124
Inches								
Bust	32	34	36	38	40	42	44	46
Waist	25	27	29	31	33	35	37	39
Hips	35	37	39	41	43	45	47	49

Relaxed-fit garments

The Drape-Front Top (see page 30), The Tie-Neck Blouse (see page 64), The Raw-Edge Coat (see page 94), and The Over-Sized T-Shirt (see page 128) are in these four sizes.

Size	1/2	3/4	5/6	7/8
Centimetres				
Bust	81-86	91-96	101-106	111-116
Waist	64-69	74-79	84-89	94-99
Hips	89-94	99-104	109-114	119-124
Inches				
Bust	32-34	36-38	40-42	44-46
Waist	25-27	29-31	33-35	37-39
Hips	35-37	39-41	43-45	47-49

Preparing to sew

If you can't find an exact match when choosing a thread to go with your fabric, opt for a slightly darker rather than lighter shade.

Iron out any incidental creases before laying out the pattern pieces. Always follow the grain line arrows printed on the paper pieces.

Once you have cut out the pattern pieces, but before you remove the paper, snip any notches to 5mm (¼in) and slip a stitch through any sewing points.

Note that seam allowances are 1cm (⅜in) unless otherwise stated.

If you are unfamiliar with the fabric type you are using, save the off-cuts. Use these to test straight and zigzag stitches, and buttonhole abilities. This is especially useful with stretch and jersey fabrics. If you are not a confident dressmaker, hand-tack seams first. Take your time sewing, especially curved seams, sleeve-heads and collars.

When sewing, do not try to follow the path of the needle with your eyes, but instead keep an eye on the edge of the fabric against the footplate guide; this will give you straighter seams. Always use the correct needle for the type and weight of fabric.

Reverse to make a few backstitches at the beginning and end of each seam, so that the stitching doesn't unravel later on.

THE STRETCH PENCIL SKIRT

Developing the stretch pencil skirt

When I was planning The Maker's Atelier, I knew that a stretch pencil skirt would be in the first set of patterns. It is so fundamental to my wardrobe that I also knew I would have to include it here in *The Essential Collection*.

Christian Dior designed the first pencil skirt back in 1954 as part of his H-line collection. Dior named his collections using letters of the alphabet to reference the changing silhouettes (we still use his term A-line for the flared cut it describes, as in an A-line skirt), and the H-line silhouette was the result of Dior's move away from his ground-breaking New Look, which with its tight waists and full skirts had dictated fashion from 1947 to 1950. The H-line shifted the emphasis from the waist to the hip, tailoring the skirt to curve over the hips and narrow towards the knee. This silhouette not only looked different, it felt radically different to wear. The more restrictive shape encouraged women to walk with a wiggle – think Marilyn Monroe in *Some Like It Hot*.

Since the 1950s, the pencil skirt with its tailored smartness has become a key piece in women's working wardrobes. Through the decades the hemline has risen and fallen, depending on the prevailing trends and the economics of the day.

In the 1970s, elastomeric fibres (best known under the trade name of Lycra) became more widely used in fabric production, adding stretch and recovery properties to both knitted and woven fabrics. These fibres have been the single biggest influence on modern dress. Without them we would not have the whole sports and leisurewear industry, with garments that cross from the gym to everyday casualwear. Tight-fitting clothing is no longer restrictive but flexes and moves with the body, allowing the wearer much greater ease of movement.

My pencil skirt is a contemporary, stretch version of the classic pencil skirt. I find rigid, tailored pencil skirts too restrictive and uncomfortable, even on a 'thin' day! This stretch version doesn't restrict my movement in the same way, but it does make me aware of how I stand and move and as a result I think it improves my posture.

The fit I like to achieve is snug over the hips, but not so tight that it becomes unflattering. Then the fabric's stretch qualities allow the skirt to follow the line of the leg without the need for a kick pleat, so giving a really clean silhouette.

At the last count I have a staggering twenty-five versions of this skirt in my personal wardrobe. They cross from casual to formal through to eveningwear; the common denominator is the stretch element in the fabrication. As this skirt takes less than a metre of fabric and a couple of hours to make, I find I can't resist great stretch fabrics that I come across when I'm fabric buying. As long as there is enough stretch I know I can create a fool-proof skirt that I will wear time and again.

How to wear the stretch pencil skirt

A stretch pencil skirt may not seem like a very forgiving garment, but it's all a question of how you wear it. I never do top-to-toe fitted with a cinched-in waist; I don't have the body or the inclination to be that obvious. A little bit of subtlety can be far more alluring. I like to balance the trim lines of the skirt with a fuller, fluid top.

Top left

The stretch pencil skirt in sparkling sequins (see also page 28) is gorgeous for evening or special occasions. Complement the shimmering effect of the skirt with a matte-finish fabric, such as this silk crinkle drape-front top (see also page 42). Finish your look with some statement earrings and a cashmere shawl for a striking sophisticated style. Head-to-toe tonal colour is a great way to add visual height and minimise those body imperfections we all think we have.

Top right

For a semi-smart everyday look, recreate the pencil skirt in a stretch woven fabric (see also page 26). The elastomeric content lessens the amount of creases compared to most non-stretch fabrics, so you feel un-crumpled and smart all day long. Wear the skirt with a cotton version of the tie-neck blouse (see also page 72) to look super efficient, or simply team it up with a knit top. The darker colour on the bottom half adds to that capable demeanour by making you look more 'grounded'.

Bottom left

I love my metallic stretch skirts, but to balance that look-at-me shine, I wear mine with a simple crew-neck sweater or classic t-shirt. The softness of a fine knit top offsets the hard metallic edge of the skirt (see also page 18), while the hint of pink adds an unexpected subtlety to that hot copper colour. Accessorise with kitten heels and, if you have the legs, add even more attitude with a pair of ankle socks.

Bottom right

Mix in those sportswear influences by teaming the skirt with a coordinating bomber jacket. This version of the pencil skirt is made in a matte-finish, coated technical jersey (see also page 28). It is worn here with the Sport-Luxe Bomber from The Maker's Atelier pattern range (see page 142). The bat-wing styling made up here in a fluid satin crepe retains a feminine edge while working that ath-leisure look. Again, keeping to tones of the same colour makes the most of the contrasting fabric textures. This is sophisticated sportswear with an urban attitude.

Technical information

The skirt

This version of the classic pencil skirt is made in a stretch fabric for a close but comfortable fit.

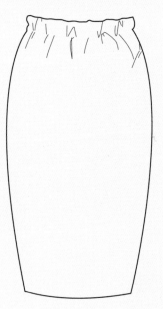

Front

Back

Sizing

Measure yourself accurately (see page 14), and check your measurements against the size chart on page 15. The chart below gives the finished sizes of the garment, so select the size that works with your measurements. Make notes where you differ from the given measurements and if need be, transfer the changes to your pattern pieces. For more on fitting patterns, turn to page 14.

Size	1	2	3	4	5	6	7	8
Centimetres								
Waist	63	68	73	78	83	88	93	98
Hips	87	92	97	102	107	112	117	122
Length from waist	69	69	69	69	69	69	69	69
Inches								
Waist	24½	26½	28½	30½	32½	34½	36½	38½
Hips	34	36	38	40	41	43	45	47
Length from waist	27	27	27	27	27	27	27	27

Fabric

This skirt can be made in stretch woven fabric and jersey knit fabric, but check the stretch and recovery: 20cm (8in) of fabric should stretch to 25cm (10in), and then return to shape when released. Ideally, select fabric with at least 4% elastane content to ensure the skirt will crease less and retain its shape, even with prolonged wear and washing. Knit fabric should have enough body to easily hold its shape.

Fabric quantity

Size (width)	1	2	3	4	5	6	7	8
Metres								
120cm wide	0.80	0.80	0.80	0.80	0.80	1.60	1.60	1.60
150cm wide	0.80	0.80	0.80	0.80	0.80	0.80	0.80	0.80
Yards								
48in wide	1	1	1	1	1	2	2	2
60in wide	1	1	1	1	1	1	1	1

Also required

- Pins
- Sewing machine
- Sewing thread to match fabric
- Tailor's chalk or fabric marker
- Non-roll elastic (as below)

Size	1	2	3	4	5	6	7	8
Metres								
2.5cm wide	0.80	0.90	0.90	0.90	1.00	1.00	1.10	1.10
Yards								
1in wide	¾	1	1	1	1	1¼	1¼	1¼

Cutting guide

Layout suggestions for 120-cm (48-in) wide and 150-cm (60-in) wide fabric.
The fabric is folded in half.

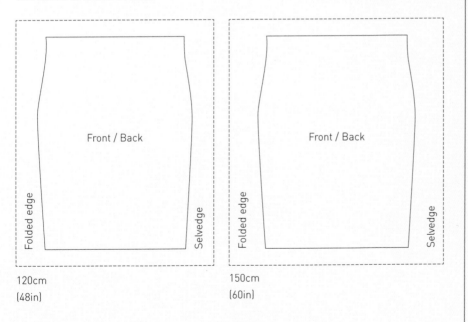

120cm
(48in)

150cm
(60in)

For sizes 6, 7 and 8 and 120-cm (48-in) wide fabric, lay out the fabric as a
single layer and cut the two pieces separately, positioning one above the other
on the fabric.

Sewing notes

Use a ballpoint needle with all
stretch fabrics. This type of needle
pushes the threads aside as
you stitch, rather than breaking
them, which you don't want with
elastane fabrics.

If you are using a PVC fabric, like
the copper metallic PVC shown
on page 17, use a Teflon presser
foot so that the fabric does not stick.

I prefer to use a straight stitch –
rather than a stretch stitch – on
side seams, just applying a little
tension as I feed the fabric through
the sewing machine. This way I get
a smoother seam and the stitches
don't break when the skirt is worn.

To make the stretch pencil skirt

Step 1

Cut out the skirt pieces, notching the edges as marked. Pin the two pieces right-sides together and stitch the side seams with a straight stitch (see Sewing Notes, page 23), 1cm (⅜in) from the edges.

At this stage you can check the fit. Slip the unfinished skirt on, inside-out so that you can pin it. If it is too loose, pin evenly on each side to the fit you would like; remember you still need to be able to walk and move! Re-stitch the seams.

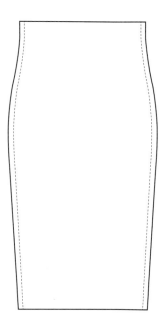

Step 2

If you are using a woven stretch fabric, either use an overlocker to neaten the seam allowances, or zigzag stitch between the side-seam stitch line and the fabric edge; this will prevent fraying. Then overlock or zigzag stitch around the waist and hem edges. This is not necessary for jersey or PVC fabrics.

Step 3

Fold the top of the skirt over at the upper notch and pin in place. Using a stretch or narrow zigzag stitch, stitch the waistband down, sewing 1cm (⅜in) from the neatened edge to create a channel for the elastic. Leave a 5cm (2½in) gap in the sewing at one of the side seams so that you can insert the elastic.

Step 4

Wrap the elastic around your waist so that it's a snug fit, and mark where the ends overlap with chalk or a fabric marker. Thread the elastic through the channel using an elastic threader or large safety pin to work the elastic round. Pin the loose end to the skirt or you could lose it into the channel and have to redo this step.

Once the elastic is threaded right through the channel, make sure it isn't twisted. Then overlap the ends of the elastic to the mark you made previously, and stitch through the layers several times to make sure they are secure. Trim off any excess, then stitch the gap in the waist channel closed.

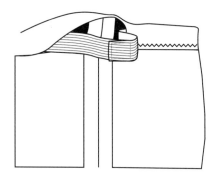

Step 5

Try on the skirt and mark the hem at the length you require. If you are using a stretch PVC fabric, you can cut the hem and leave it raw-edged as it doesn't fray. However, you must remember to secure the ends of the side seams with a few hand-stitches to prevent them unravelling where they have been cut.

Alternatively, turn up and pin the hem to the required length, then use one of the hem finishes shown on pages 28–29.

If appropriate for the fabric, lightly press the skirt on the wrong side, using a cool iron or pressing cloth. Turn the skirt right-side out and it's ready to wear.

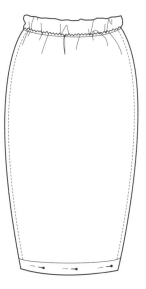

Making more of the stretch pencil skirt

The basic pattern for this skirt is easy to adapt to create different looks. Rather than cutting up the original pattern, trace it on to dressmaker's tissue and keep the original intact for future projects.

Seam detailing

This seam detailing idea encourages the eye to run down the garment for a visually slimming effect. The seams also break up the plain front and back.

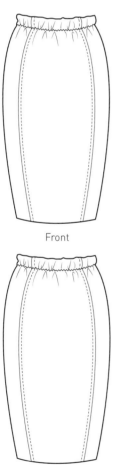

Front

Back

Step 1

Trace a new pattern from the basic pattern. Trim a strip 9cm (3½in) wide from each side; the remaining piece is the new centre panel for the front and the back. Cut two rectangles 20 x 75cm (8 x 29½in) in the same fabric; these are the new side panels.

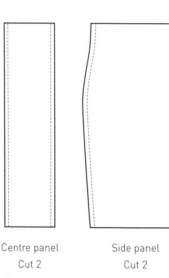

Centre panel
Cut 2

Side panel
Cut 2

Step 2

Join the four pieces together to create the skirt tube. If you are using a woven stretch fabric, overlock or zigzag stitch the seam allowances. Press all the seam allowances to the middle of the skirt. On the right side of the fabric, topstitch the seam allowances 3mm (⅛in) in from the seam line. Then overlock or zigzag stitch around the waist and hem edges.

Step 3

Follow Steps 3–5 on pages 24–25 to finish the seam detail skirt.

Panel colour blocking

You can expand the seam detailing idea further and incorporate colour blocking. Use a darker colour for the side panels to heighten the visual slimming effect in a way that's stylish and contemporary.

Step 1

Create a pattern as for the seam detail skirt (see above), but cut out the side panels in a contrast or complementary colour to the centre panels. Then follow the steps to make up the skirt.

Front

Back

Hem finishes

Sewing with stretch fabrics can be tricky, and hems can prove to be the most difficult area to get right. The aim is to have a smooth stitch and fabric finish, but with enough stretch to be able to move in the garment without the stitches breaking.

Here are some suggestions for different hem finishes; to make sure you choose the best one, try these out on fabric offcuts before working on your skirt.

Top left: Sequin fabric skirt hemmed with simple zigzag stitch.
Top right: Seam detail skirt hemmed using twin needle stitch.
Bottom left: Satin skirt with a scallop hem.
Bottom right: Technical jersey fabric skirt hemmed using fusible hemming strip.

Simple zigzag stitch

Suitable for most single jersey constructions, the zigzag stitch stretches with the fabric as you walk. If you find that the fabric splays out or puckers with this technique, try altering the stitch width and length until the fabric lies flat.

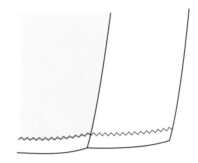

Twin needle stitch

Suggested for lighter-weight jersey fabrics, this produces two neat lines of parallel straight stitch on the right side, but with a zigzag on the reverse to allow the fabric to stretch without the stitching breaking.

Fit the twin needle in the sewing machine and thread it up according to your user manual. Hand-tack the hem in place and then, on the right side of the fabric, stitch around the hem, making sure the stitch line stays parallel to the hem and is firmly securing both layers.

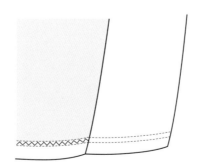

Scallop hem

This is a great finish for stretch satins and other high-sheen fabrics that can splay out.

Instead of sewing around the hem, fold the hem up and secure it in place with vertical lines of stitching. Make the lines equal length and approximately 3cm (1¼in) apart.

You can use a similar effect on the Seam Detail version of the skirt (see page 26). If you don't want the hem to show at all, simply fold it up and then stitch it in place by stitching through the seam lines. Press the hem on the wrong side using a pressing cloth.

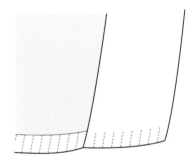

Fusible hemming strip

This is a rather last-resort option, as it's not very permanent on stretch fabrics because it can break. The lighter weight fusible strip is more flexible, and you must carefully follow the manufacturer's instructions for the type of fabric you are using.

THE DRAPE-FRONT TOP

Developing the drape-front top

This is one of my favourite tops to wear with my stretch pencil skirts
(see page 16); the soft, fluid lines complement the sharp shape of the skirt.
For the same reason, it's also a great top to wear under a tailored jacket.
It's a simple shape that has evolved through years of playing around with
fabric – especially jersey fabric – and learning how it drapes.

I've always loved jersey, but when I first started sewing I found it tricky to work
with. I didn't know about ballpoint needles, and my mother's ancient old
Singer sewing machine didn't have a zigzag stitch. The clunky straight stitch
flattened the fabric out, and then the stitching round the neck would break.

My first successful jersey garment was a slash-neck tube with side slits
made in a double jersey. This denser fabric was easier to sew with, but even
then to create the slash neck, I simply turned the edge under and loosely
slip-stitched it in place.

What I really wanted was to be able to use lighter weight, single jersey fabrics
that draped. I had a cowl-neck sweater and thought I'd take that idea and
translate it into single jersey fabric. The problem was I thought I needed to
finish the neck edge to stop the fabric from fraying, and when I did that, I lost
the draped quality. Of course, the more I experimented the more I learned,
and once I was given my own sewing machine – with a zigzag function – sewing
with jersey became much easier.

But what really made me think about how I work with fabric was seeing what
the designer Alber Elbaz was creating for Lanvin. At first glance the clothes
were understated, almost low-key – except for the quality of the fabrics.
He really allows the fabrics to work with the body; he drapes and tucks while
retaining a fluid, body-skimming fit, and I find this more attractive than fitted,
body-conscious styles. With more structured fabrics, he was cutting simpler,
boxy shapes, and also leaving some of these incredibly luxurious fabrics with
raw, fraying edges. That was the first time I'd seen this treatment and initially
I was shocked that a dress or coat costing hundreds of pounds could be left
'unfinished'. But then I realised this added to the beauty of what Alber was
creating: he was challenging what luxury meant. I decided to invest in more
expensive fabrics and see how they would hang, not worrying about finishing
any edges, just letting the fabric do the work. Alber Elbaz's inspiration
freed-up my design process.

I was fortunate enough to be given a proper dressmaking mannequin by
one of the companies I designed for, so I just started pinning fabric to see how
it fell, and then created a style from there. This is how I developed my first
unstructured, raw-edged draped top.

That top has now evolved into the Drape-Front Top featured here. It can work
across jersey and woven fabrics through subtle alteration to the width of
the front, and both front pattern pieces are included in the pattern envelope.

How to wear the drape-front top

This is a very feminine top to wear and one of my favourites when worn with a pencil skirt and tailored jacket; the fluid lines complement those more structured garments. The soft folds around the neckline are flattering in a way a basic round neck can be harder to pull-off, especially if it isn't exactly the right curve to suit your body and face.

Top left

In its simplest form, this is the drape-front top in a subtly textured viscose jersey (see also page 32). It's as easy to pull on as a t-shirt, but with a much more feminine edge. Pair it with the stretch pencil skirt (see also page 16) for an easy everyday look. Then layer on some accessories to take you from day to night. The warm creamy white colour of the jersey gives this top a more luxurious feel. Try to avoid cold bluish whites in jersey fabrics as they rarely flatter any skin tone.

Top right

For a workwear option, choose the double-layer drape-front top (see also page 41). The additional layer increases the top's weight and drape, disguising any lumps and bumps you don't want to show! Here it is worn with the lined version of the wrap skirt (see also page 124) in a discreet checked wool for a smart but not too formal business look. Darker, more neutral tones give an air of authority to the wearer; adopt these if you want to be taken seriously.

Bottom left

This light-as-a-feather, crinkle-silk crepe is perfect for the woven version of this top (see also page 42). It is a great example of how I like the fabric to do the work; the looser shape of the woven front lets the fabric move as you do. I like to wear this version of the drape-front top with the cigarette pants (see also page 46) or a more casual version of the pencil skirt. I feel all that fluidity needs the anchor of a tougher, more masculine piece of clothing to show it off. To ring the changes, why not add a decorative pin to the front, as shown on page 4.

Bottom right

Adding a drawstring to the drape-front top does accentuate one's curves (see also page 44). Try this top as an alternative to more traditional eveningwear for a great night out. The blush-coloured silk crepe is trimmed with a stretch, metallic copper drawstring, which coordinates well with the metallic stretch pencil skirt (see also page 18) to create just enough bling.

Technical information

The top

This relaxed fit, pull-on, sleeveless top has a softly draped front and a smooth back.

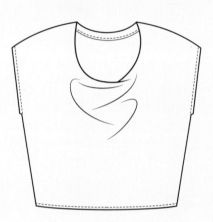

Front

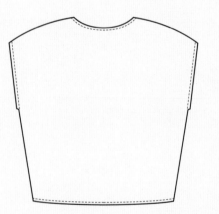

Back

Sizing

Measure yourself accurately (see page 14), and check your measurements against the size chart on page 15. The chart below gives the finished sizes of the garment, so select the size that works with your measurements (remembering that garments are designed with ease to make them fit comfortably). Make notes where you differ from the given measurements and if need be, transfer the changes to your pattern pieces. For more on fitting patterns, turn to page 14.

Size	1/2	3/4	5/6	7/8
Centimetres				
Bust	115	125	135	145
Hips	107	117	127	137
Length from side neck	59	60	61	62
Overarm from side neck to sleeve edge	27	29	31	33
Inches				
Bust	45	49	53	57
Hips	42	46	50	54
Length from side neck	23¼	23½	23¾	24
Overarm from side neck to sleeve edge	10¾	11½	12¼	13

Fabric

This top is best made in fluid, jersey fabric and the pattern instructions reflect that. However, with a little alteration it can be made in some silky, woven fabrics (see Making More Of The Draped-Front Top Pattern, page 41).

Fabric quantity

Size	1/2	3/4	5/6	7/8
Metres				
120/150cm wide	1.40	1.40	1.40	1.40
Yards				
48/60in wide	1½	1½	1½	1½

Cutting guide

Layout suggestion for 120/150-cm (48/60-in) wide fabric. The fabric is folded in half.

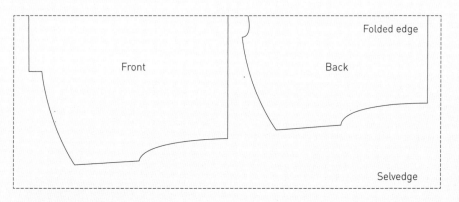

Sewing notes

Seam allowances are 1cm (⅜in) unless otherwise stated.

When sewing with jersey fabrics, always use a ballpoint or jersey needle. Stitch using a straight stitch, but apply a slight tension to the fabric as you feed it through; this will mean that your seam is less likely to break when the fabric stretches.

Also required

- Fabric scissors
- Pins
- Iron and ironing board
- Sewing machine
- Sewing thread to match fabric
- 30cm (12in) of 12-mm (½-in) wide bias binding

To make the drape-front top

Step 1

Cut out the top pieces, cutting 5mm (¼in) notches as marked.

Step 2

Open out one side of the bias binding. Right-sides together, pin the binding along the back neck, matching the raw edges of the binding and fabric. Then stitch along the fold line, taking care not to stretch the fabric or binding as you go (a).

Fold the binding over to the wrong side of the back piece, folding over 3mm (⅛in) of fabric as well. Pin and then stitch along the lower edge of the binding, again taking care not to stretch it or the fabric (b).

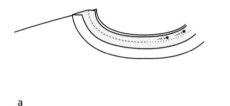

a

b

Step 3

Place the front and back pieces right-sides together and pin them from shoulder to neck. Stitch the seams and press the seam allowances open using a pressing cloth.

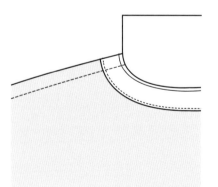

Step 4

At the side neck, turn under the edge of the facing to just cover the shoulder seam. Fold it to the wrong side and tack it in place, being careful not to stretch it. On the right side, stitch through the shoulder seam to secure the facing in position. Then remove the tacking stitches.

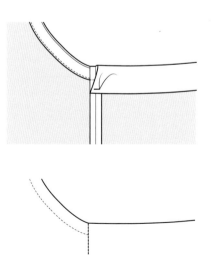

Step 5

With the front and back pieces right-sides together and working from the hem to the underarm, pin the side seam on both sides. Stitch the seam and press the seam allowances open using a pressing cloth.

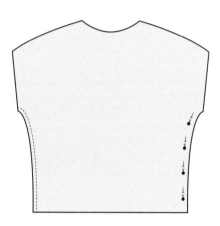

Step 6

Turn under the sleeve edge by 1cm (⅜in) and pin in place. Using a zigzag stitch or stretch stitch, stitch the hem in place.

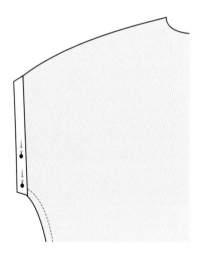

Step 7

As with the sleeves, turn under a 1cm (⅜in) bottom edge hem, pin and then stitch it using a zigzag or stretch stitch.

Press the top and it is ready to wear.

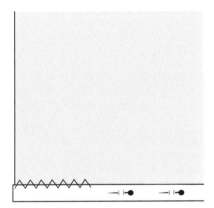

Making more of the drape-front top pattern

Double-layer top

This is ideal if you have found a jersey fabric that you love the colour of, but that is a little bit too thin. You will need to buy twice the listed fabric quantity.

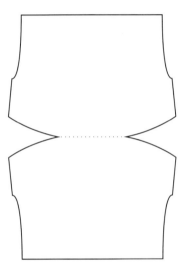

Front

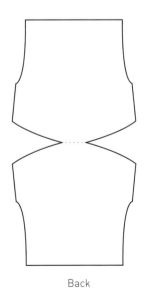

Back

Step 1
Lay the pattern pieces on the fabric. Using tailor's chalk, draw around each pattern piece from one neck point round to the other neck point. On the imaginary line between the neck points, flip the pattern piece over to mirror the drawn shape and draw around it again. Cut out the double front as one piece and the double back as one piece, as shown on the left.

Step 2
Fold the shapes in half with the wrong sides together. Now make up the top following Step 3 then Steps 5–7 on pages 38–39.

Working with double layers of fabric

Having multiple layers of fabric can cause problems when stitching seams, as the layers can 'creep' – can move at different speeds under the presser foot – and so you end up with uneven length seams. There are a few solutions you can try to solve this.

You can put in a lot of pins along the seam lines, putting them in horizontally rather than vertically to hold the layers firmly.

You can hand-tack all the seams, using a fairly small tacking stitch, and then machine-stitch them.

An expensive option, so not one to try if you do not sew regularly, is to buy a special walking foot for your sewing machine, which will help feed all the layers of fabric through evenly.

Woven fabric drape-front top

You need to use the front pattern piece designed for woven fabric, though the back pattern piece is the same as for jersey fabric. To let the front neck drape correctly the fabric needs to be left with raw edges. You will need a fabric that is fluid with plenty of drape; linens and tweeds are not a good idea.

Front

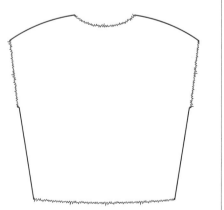

Back

Step 1

For a perfect frayed edge, start by making a small snip at the selvedge near the top of the fabric; leave enough fabric above the snip to get a grip on. Tear the fabric across the width. Fray the edge by pulling out a few rows of warp threads (the threads that run across the fabric). If you are concerned that the fabric won't tear, cut off a small piece and experiment with that before tearing the main length.

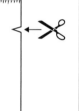

Step 2

If the fabric won't tear, ease out a thread from the warp, either in the selvedge or close to it. Gently pull the thread, ruching up the fabric as you go and pulling until the thread breaks; it should leave a fine line in the fabric. Carefully cut along this line. Fray the edge in the same way as for torn fabric.

Step 3

Place the neck edge of the front pattern piece against the frayed edge. Mark the bottom edge of the pattern piece, then tear or cut along the marked line to create a frayed bottom edge. At the sleeve edges, either use pinking shears or cut the fabric straight then slightly fray the edge by carefully pulling out some threads. Cut out the back piece in the same way.

Step 4

If you are worried that the material will keep on fraying too much for your liking, you can run a small zigzag stitch near the frayed edge. However, if you are using a crinkle fabric, as in the photograph, this is not advisable as it will flatten and stretch out the fabric.

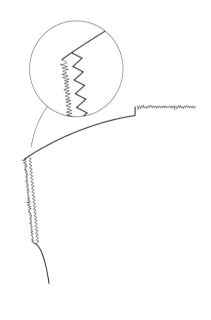

Step 5

Once the pieces are prepared, place them right-sides together and pin and then stitch the shoulder seams. Do the same with the side seams. Press the seam allowances open using a pressing cloth. If you are using a crinkle fabric, just steam – rather then press – the seam allowances open.

Drawstring neck top

This variation is made in a woven fabric, and in addition to the fabric you will need 1m (39in) of 12mm (½in) bias binding, 120cm (48in) of cord elastic, and 3cm (1¼in) square of fusible interfacing.

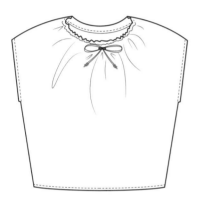

Step 1

Cut out the front and back pieces, using the woven fabric front pattern piece.

The drawstring neck requires a buttonhole opening 2cm (¾in) long at the centre front, 5mm (¼in) down from the finished neck edge. Firstly, mark the centre front point with tailor's chalk. Place the 3cm (1¼in) square of fusible interlining on the wrong side of the fabric, centrally on the top of the neck edge. Iron it in place using a pressing cloth.

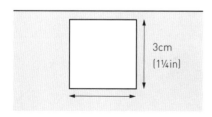

3cm
(1¼in)

Step 2

On the right side of the interfaced section of fabric, draw a chalk line 2cm (¾in) long, 1.75cm (⅝in) down from the neck edge and parallel to it. Using buttonhole stitch or tight satin stitch, work a buttonhole around this line, then carefully snip it open.

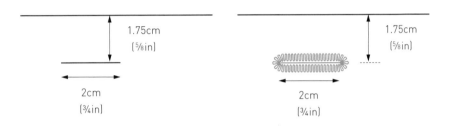

Step 3

Pin the front and back right-sides together at the shoulder seams, stitch the seams and press the seam allowances open. Do the same at the side seams.

Step 4

Stay stitch around the neckline 5mm (¼in) from the edge to ensure it doesn't stretch out of shape. Open out one side of the bias binding. Right-sides together, pin the binding right around the neck, matching the raw edges of the binding and fabric. Overlap the ends of the binding by 1cm (⅜in) and trim off any excess. Then stitch along the fold line, taking care not to stretch the fabric or binding as you go.

Fold the binding over to the wrong side of the back piece, folding over 3mm (⅛in) of fabric as well. Pin and then stitch along the lower edge of the binding to form the channel for the drawstring.

Step 5

Turn under hem and sleeve edges over by 5mm (¼in) and press. Then turn under a further 1cm (⅜in) and press. Pin and then stitch the hems in place.

Step 6

Thread the cord elastic through the channel. Try the top on and tie the drawstring to where it feels comfortable; note that there is no gathering across the back neck of the top. Finish the ends with a little knot and a bow, or a loop.

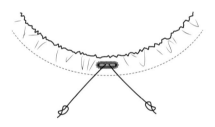

THE CIGARETTE PANTS

Developing the cigarette pants

Trousers are such a fundamental item in most women's wardrobes today that it's odd to think that it's only since the late 1950s that they have been part of mainstream fashion for women of all ages.

Working women started wearing trousers for light industrial and agricultural work in the early 20th century. During the two World Wars this movement grew, with many women adapting their absent husband's trousers to wear for work in the munitions factories.

But it was pioneering female aviators such as Amelia Earhart and Amy Johnson who brought a sense of style to this emerging trend.

By the 1930s, Hollywood actresses Katharine Hepburn and Greta Garbo were regularly photographed wearing trousers, encouraging more women to do so in their leisure time. In the May 1939 edition of British *Vogue*, the editorial 'The Case For Slacks' urged the fashionable, modern woman to wear slacks 'practically the whole time'.

Up until the 1950s, trousers remained loose fitting, but then the silhouette slimmed right down to what became known as Capri Pants. This was before the invention of elastane, so these early slim-line trousers were lined to prevent bagging around the seat and knees.

But by the time Alexander McQueen showed his infamous Bumster trousers in 2003, most narrow-legged trousers were made from stretch fabric, making them more comfortable to wear. Adding elastomeric yarn to woven fabrics also made it possible for mass-produced trousers to actually fit.

Trends in trouser shapes have always moved much more slowly than skirt or dress shapes. The current trend for slim-fit trousers – including skinny jeans and leggings – has been with us for more than a decade, and our wardrobes are built around balancing the proportions of the thin leg with longer-line tunic tops and looser parka or box-style coats, effectively ignoring the waist. Adding wide-legged trousers to that wardrobe makes the whole look become loose and slouchy, which can be unflattering. So to move towards the wider-legged trouser that's becoming more popular, means changing the overall silhouette by investing in styles to balance out the wider bottom half. This will take some time.

So the trouser I have selected for *The Essential Collection* is this Cigarette Pant. The pattern has evolved over time as I have refined the fit and line. Unlike McQueen's Bumsters, this trouser sits on the waist and fits from the hip to mid-thigh, then skims the leg, giving the appearance of a narrow parallel leg or cigarette shape, hence the name.

How to wear the cigarette pants

If you like wearing trousers, then these are a great versatile addition
to your wardrobe. This cigarette pant is just such an easy trouser
style to wear; the stretch elastane content adds to the comfort and
look of the garment. Shown here in plain colours, this style could also
work well in a small checked or jacquard patterned weave.

Top left

Cropped or Capri pants (see also page 62) can make your legs look shorter,
so I prefer to accessorise mine with a kitten heel – this adds a bit of
height and accentuates my ankles. I also like to wear these trousers with
a version of the raw-edge coat (see also page 109) or The Over-Sized
Shirtdress from The Maker's Atelier pattern range (see page 142).

Top right

These trousers are ideal as a working wardrobe staple. Slim but not too
skinny-legged, wear them with the tie-front blouse for a smarter look:
a print blouse adds colour and pattern (see also page 77). Stick to darker
neutrals for more versatility, and black if you want the trousers to go
with almost anything. Depending on how formal you wish to look, a sheen
finish to your fabric will look more polished than casual brushed cotton.

Bottom left

Mix luxury fabrics in a head-to-toe pastel shade for a sophisticated take
on the smart-casual look. The pin-tuck seam detail (see also page 61)
adds a sharper edge to these Ponte Roma cigarette pants. Team them
up with a silk satin blouse and a cashmere crew to complete the look.
This blouse is a version of The Box Shirt from The Maker's Atelier pattern
range (see page 142).

Bottom right

What could be easier than pulling on a stretch cigarette pant and an
over-sized t-shirt (see also page 128) or sweater? Here the basic cigarette
pants are in a textured stretch herringbone weave that works well when
teamed with a coordinating striped top (see also page 130). Add a rolled
turn-up and a great pair of loafers for a bit of continental attitude:
how to look stylishly relaxed all weekend.

Technical information

The pants

These trousers sit on the waist and fit from the hip to mid-thigh, then skim the leg.

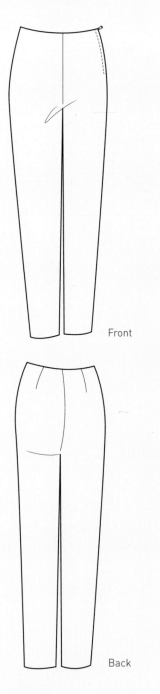

Front

Back

Sizing

A great fit for trousers can be difficult to achieve first time around when making your own, so I strongly recommend that you make a toile first to achieve the perfect fit for you (see page 15).

Measure yourself accurately (see page 14), and check your measurements against the size chart on page 15. The chart below gives the finished sizes of the garment, so select the size that works with your measurements (remembering that garments are designed with ease to make them fit comfortably). Make notes where you differ from the given measurements and if need be, transfer the changes to your pattern pieces. For more on fitting patterns, turn to page 14.

Size	1	2	3	4	5	6	7	8
Centimetres								
Waist	64	70.5	77	83.5	90	96.5	103	109.5
Hips	89	95.5	102	108.5	115	121.5	128	134.5
Inside leg	80	80	80	80	80	80	80	80
CF drop	23.5	24.5	25	25.75	26.25	27.25	28	28.75
CB drop	33	34	34.5	35	36	37	38	38.5
Inches								
Waist	25¼	27¾	30¼	32¾	35¼	37¾	40¼	42¾
Hips	35	37½	40	42½	45	47½	50	52½
Inside leg	31	31	31	31	31	31	31	31
CF drop	9½	9¾	10	10¼	10½	10¾	11	11¼
CB drop	13	13½	13¾	14	14¼	14½	14¾	15

Fabric

These trousers can be made in stretch woven fabrics and some double knit jersey fabrics, for example a Ponte Roma construction. But all fabrics must contain at least 4% elastane for your trousers to retain their shape.

Fabric quantity

Size	1	2	3	4	5	6	7	8
Metres								
120cm wide	2.20	2.20	2.20	2.20	2.20	2.20	2.20	2.20
150cm wide	1.30	1.30	1.30	1.30	1.30	1.30	1.30	1.30
Yards								
48in wide	2½	2½	2½	2½	2½	2½	2½	2½
60in wide	1½	1½	1½	1½	1½	1½	1½	1½

Also required

- Fabric scissors
- Pins
- Iron and ironing board
- Sewing machine
- Sewing thread to match fabric
- Hand-sewing needle
- 20cm (8in) zip
- Hook-and-eye fastening
- Fusible woven interfacing (as per below)

Size	1	2	3	4	5	6	7	8
Metres								
120/150cm wide	0.30	0.30	0.30	0.30	0.30	0.30	0.30	0.30
Yards								
48/60in wide	⅓	⅓	⅓	⅓	⅓	⅓	⅓	⅓

Cutting guide

Layout suggestions for 120-cm (48-in) wide fabric. The fabric is folded in half.

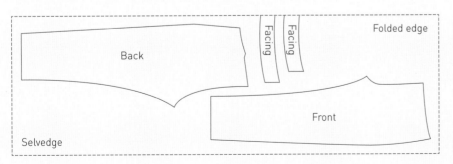

Cutting guide

Layout suggestions for 150-cm (60-in) wide fabric. The fabric is folded in half.

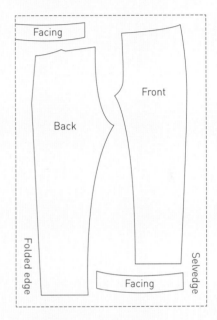

Sewing notes

Seam allowances are 1cm (⅜in) unless otherwise stated.

To avoid fraying seams, overlock or zigzag stitch all the cut-out garment pieces before constructing the trousers. As a last resort use pinking shears, but increase the seam allowances by 5mm (¼in).

Use a ballpoint needle with all stretch fabrics. This type of needle pushes the threads aside as you stitch, rather than breaking them.

I prefer to use a straight stitch – rather than a stretch stitch – on seams, just applying a little tension as I feed the fabric through the machine. This gives a smoother seam and the stitches don't break when the trousers are worn.

To make the cigarette pants

Step 1

Cut out the trouser pieces, cutting 5mm (¼in) notches as marked. Make a small hand-stitch at the point of the dart on each back piece.

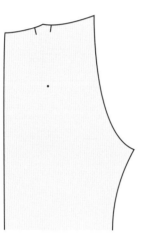

Step 2

Right-side in, fold each trouser back piece so that the two dart notches meet and the fold line goes down to the dart point marked by the hand-stitch. Pin in place, then machine-stitch a straight line down from the notch to the point (see Sewing Notes, page 53), making sure you stitch just beyond the point. Leave long thread ends at the point that you can knot to make sure the dart stitching is secure. Press the darts towards the centre back.

 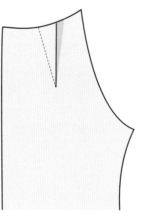

Step 3

Place the two trouser backs right-sides together and pin then stitch the centre back seam. Repeat with the two front pieces to stitch the centre front seam. Press the seams open.

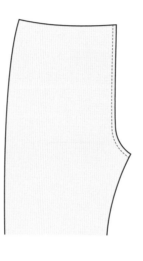

Step 4

Place the front and back of the trousers right-sides together. On the left-hand side as you look at the trousers, stitch from the notch that is 22cm (8¾in) from the top, down to the hem. Then lengthen the machine stitch to as long as it will go and stitch from the notch to the top of the trousers; do not fasten off the threads as you will be removing these stitches later.

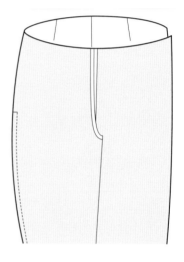

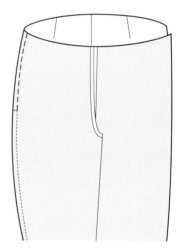

Step 5

On the wrong side of the fabric and using a pressing cloth, press the seam allowances open (a).

Place the zip face-down on the seam, matching the teeth with the stitch line and with the endstop of the zip 1mm (¹⁄₁₆in) below the notch (b). Pin the zip in place.

Using a zip foot, stitch the zip in place, stitching down one side of the tape and then across the bottom of the zip just below the endstop. Go back to the top and stitch down the other side of the tape (c).

Remove the long stitches that run from the notch to the top, and test the zip to make sure it opens smoothly without catching on the fabric (d).

Zips and setting them

There are two types of zip you can use for these trousers, a standard zip or an invisible zip. Standard zips can be set in lapped or centred, and invisible zips can be set using either of those styles, or invisibly. I like the look of invisible zips and so tend to use them, but I usually use a centred setting, as here, rather than an invisible setting.

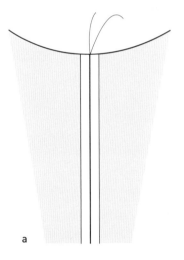

a

b

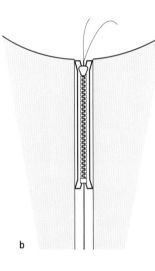

c

d

Step 6

Change the presser foot back to a standard one. Pin and stitch the seam on the right-hand side of the trousers, stitching from top to hem. Press the seam allowances open, again on the wrong side of the fabric and using a pressing cloth.

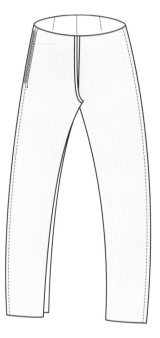

Step 7

Working from the crotch to the hem, pin the inside leg seam on both sides. Stitch from the hem on one side all the way round to the hem on the other side. Press this seam open, again on the wrong side of the fabric and using a pressing cloth.

At this stage slip the trousers on and make any alterations as necessary.

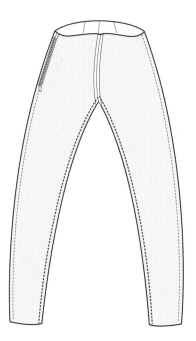

Step 8

Iron the interfacing pieces onto the wrong side of the trouser facing pieces. Check the interfaced pieces against the pattern pieces and trim them if necessary.

Pin the front and back facing pieces right-sides together and stitch the right-hand side seam as shown (a). Press the seam open.

Turn the trousers right-side out and place the facing, right-side down, around the trouser top, matching the top edge of the facing with the top edge of the trousers (b).

Pin from the right-hand side seam (the side without the zip) around to the zip – there should be 1cm (⅜in) of the facing overhanging the edge of the zip setting on each side. If not, ease the facing to achieve this (c).

Stitch the facing to the trousers starting from one side of the zip and going right around to the other side (d).

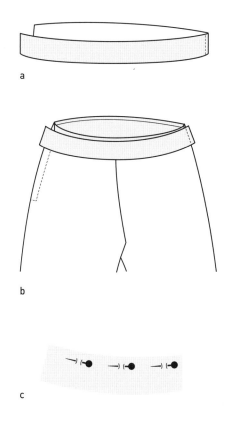

a

b

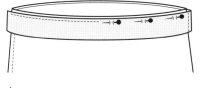

c

d

Step 9

Turn the trousers wrong-side out. Fold the facing to the inside, so the seam is just 1mm (¹⁄₁₆in) below the fold line, and press it in place. Turn under the 1cm (³⁄₈in) overhanging the zip on each side, making sure that the zip teeth are clear of the fabric, and stitch it down, as shown. Turn the trousers back to the right-side out and topstitch for 4cm (1½in) down the other side seam, the centre front and back seams, and down the dart lines to catch the facing in place.

Hand-stitch the hook-and-eye fastening to the top of the waistband, just above the zip.

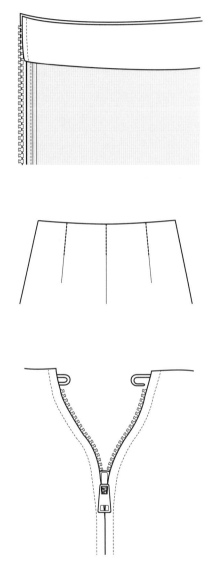

Step 10

Once again, turn the trousers wrong-side out and slip them on. Turn up the legs to the length you require and pin in place. Carefully slip the trousers off.

Check that both trouser legs are the same length and then stitch the hems in place, either by machine or by hand.

Give the trousers a final press, turn them right-side out, and they are ready to wear.

Making more of the cigarette pants

Cigarette pants with pin-tuck seam detail

This is a great detail if you like your clothes to look smart.

Step 1

On the pattern piece for the front trouser leg there is a dotted line running down the centre; make a small notch in the fabric at the top and bottom of this line.

Step 2

Before starting to make up the trousers, fold each front leg piece, right-side out, along this line and pin the layers flat. Stitch 3mm (⅛in) from the fold all the way along, making sure the line of stitching remains straight. Press the pieces on the wrong side, then make up the trousers as instructed following the steps on pages 54–59.

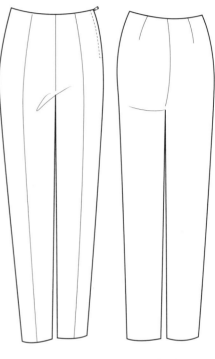

Front   Back

Topstitching tucks

It takes some practice to be able to topstitch a tiny tuck perfectly. Start by establishing where the folded edge of the fabric will run along the plate under the presser foot, and mark this line with a strip of masking tape. Then stitch slowly, keeping the edge of the fabric aligned with the edge of the tape and don't watch the needle; the up-and-down movement can upset your concentration.

Alternatively, there are excellent top-stitching presser feet available for most makes of sewing machine. Some of these enable you to not only stitch perfect pintucks, but also to topstitch edges such as necklines and patch pockets.

Capri pants

For a more sporty style, make classic Capri pants with a side-split detail.

Front   Back

Step 1

Fold back the trouser leg as marked on the front and back leg trouser pattern pieces. Cut out the shorter length trousers, making the small notch for the top of the side split.

Make up the trousers following the steps on pages 54–59, but on the outer leg seams only stitch down to the notch marking the top of the side split.

Step 2

Continue following the main instructions through to Step 9. Turn up the hems by 1cm (⅜in) then a further 8cm (3in) and press.

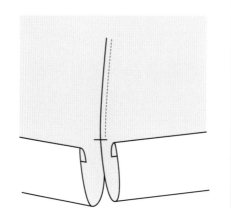

Step 3

Fold the fabric the other way along the lower hem and open out the narrow hem, so that the right sides of the fabric are flat together. On one side of the split, stitch from the hem to the end of the side seam. Carefully trim off the corner of the seam allowance, as shown. Fold this side up out of the way, then repeat the process on the other side of the split, and then on the other leg.

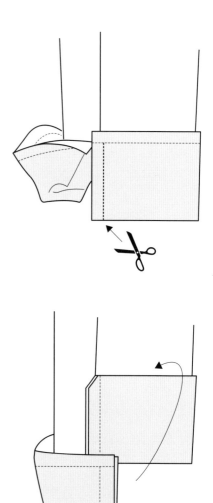

Step 4

Fold the narrow hem over again and then turn the hems right-side out. Stitch the hems in place, either by machine or by hand. Give the Capri pants a final press and they are ready to wear.

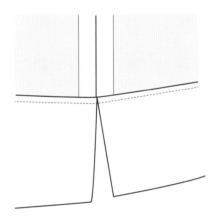

THE TIE-NECK BLOUSE

Developing the tie-neck blouse

I'm not a very blousy sort of person; I can't do girly and won't do mumsy! But there's something about a tie-neck blouse that can be chic; it's all about how you wear it.

I was lucky enough to grow up in a big family with stylish older siblings, so I inherited some great hand-me-downs. One of the treasures I acquired was a fabulous silk, pussy-bow blouse in a 30s-inspired floral print. This was a sophisticated item for a 12-year-old tomboy like me, and I wasn't really sure how to wear it at first. It looked too prissy with a skirt, but when I put it on with some Oxford bags I thought I looked the business! Looking back, this was probably my first attempt at the androgynous look, no doubt influenced by my obsession with David Bowie.

The term pussy bow has been in circulation since the 1930s and refers to the sort of bow that used to be tied around a kitten's neck. In the 1960s, Yves Saint Laurent designed some fabulous pussy-bow blouses that influenced more mainstream fashion. The look was especially popular in corporate America, where female office workers were beginning to compete in a man's world. The fluid bow feminised their austere, tailored workwear while retaining an air of professionalism. Margaret Thatcher obviously thought the style had the stamp of authority, as it became a key part of her political image.

More recently Hedi Slimane revisited the tie-neck blouse during his tenure designing the womenswear range at Yves Saint Laurent. His interpretation is definitely more rock chick than office worker; very louche with a much narrower tie and worn with his signature narrow-legged trousers. A similar interpretation can be seen in the Kate Moss collaboration with the French shirting label, Equipment. Interestingly, the softer, fuller pussy-bow blouse has now appeared in Alessandro Michele's menswear collections for Gucci. This style of blouse really can be lady-like or rock chick, prim or sassy, laid-back or uptight.

This is my interpretation of the tie-neck blouse. I wanted to avoid the prim look so I've lowered the neck to a deep V and kept the body and sleeves unstructured. The tie can be either slim and neat or deep and flouncy. It can be recreated in many ways depending on your style but I hope you'll think it chic.

How to wear the tie-neck blouse

As I mentioned earlier, with a tie-neck blouse it is all about how you wear it and the fabric you choose to make it in; soft and blousy or crisp and shirt-like. The former will without doubt be more luxe, but the latter needn't be too stiff. Here's some inspiration.

Top left

Here we have the main version of the tie-neck blouse made in a fine-count, soft cotton shirting (see also page 66) and worn simply with a pair of Capris (see also page 62) for an easy, relaxed look. The same blouse looks very different paired with the wool wrap skirt on the opening page of this chapter. The subtle mix of narrow stripe and fine check add that touch of interest to avoid looking stuffy but still look smart enough for work. Mixing pattern doesn't always have to be about the big and the bold, which is hard to pull off. Try subtler fabric choices with smaller patterns and blending colours for an easier more wearable look.

Top right

Undoubtedly the pussy-bow version of this blouse is more girly, especially when made in pastel silks (see also page 77). But try wearing it with the leather jacket (see also page 106) and cigarette pants (see also page 61) to look effortlessly cool and sophisticated. Again, here we see how pastel hues in luxury fabrics can look so special; the result is feminine and flirty but also assured.

Bottom left

This style makes for a real statement piece when created in a narrative or scarf print. Take your time getting the exact positioning you want for your print then work that look. This fine silk scarf print version (see also page 77) can be worn tucked in or out. Shown here tucked into a version of the wrap skirt (see also page 124), it would take on a more holiday look worn with a pair of the cigarette Capris (see page 62).

Bottom right

The strong contrast trim on this version of the tie-neck blouse (see also page 78) looks cool and crisp with this pigment-dyed denim wrap skirt (see also page 115). The sharp lines created by adding this trim to the tie complement the asymmetrical cut of the skirt. This is smart but certainly not frumpy. You could also try a patterned blouse fabric with a coordinating trim or vice versa; the options are endless.

Technical information

The blouse

This blouse is a relaxed fit with straight sides and a front button fastening.

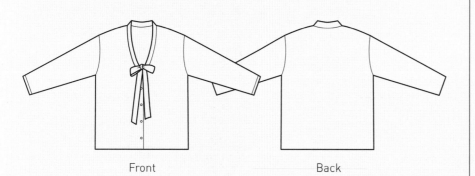

Front   Back

Fabric

This blouse can be made in most lightweight woven fabrics; cotton shirting and poplin, handkerchief linen, silk and viscose mixes.

Sizing

Measure yourself accurately (see page 14), and check your measurements against the size chart on page 15. The chart below gives the finished sizes of the garment, so select the size that works with your measurements (remembering that garments are designed with ease to make them fit comfortably). Make notes where you differ from the given measurements and if need be, transfer the changes to your pattern pieces. For more on fitting patterns, turn to page 114.

Size	1/2	3/4	5/6	7/8
Centimetres				
Bust	108	118	128	138
Hips	108	118	128	138
Length from side neck	65.75	67	68.25	69.5
Overarm from side neck to sleeve edge	74	75	76	77
Inches				
Bust	42	46	50	54
Hips	42	46	50	54
Length from side neck	25½	26	26½	27
Overarm from side neck to sleeve edge	29	29½	30	30½

Fabric quantity

Size	1/2	3/4	5/6	7/8
Metres				
120cm wide	2.20	2.20	2.20	2.20
150cm wide	1.50	1.50	1.50	1.50
Yards				
48in wide	2½	2½	2½	2½
60in wide	2	2	2	2

Cutting guide

Layout suggestions for 120-cm (48-in) wide fabric. The fabric is folded in half.

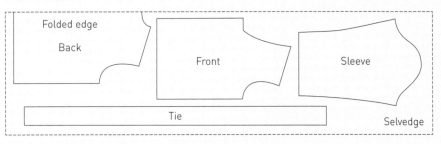

Layout suggestions for 150-cm (60-in) wide fabric. The fabric is a single layer.

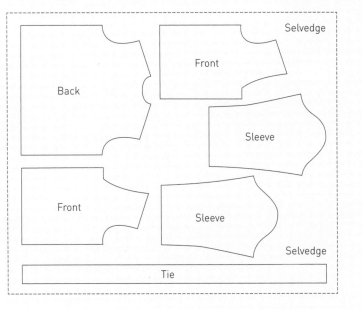

Also required

- Fabric scissors
- Pins
- Iron and ironing board
- Sewing machine
- Sewing thread to match fabric
- 5 x 10mm (⅜in) buttons
- Hand-sewing needle
- Safety pin (for turning ties right-side out)

Sewing notes

Seam allowances are 1cm (⅜in) unless otherwise stated.

To avoid fraying seams, if you own an overlocker or serger, overlock all the cut-out garment pieces before constructing the trousers. Alternatively, use the overlock stitch or zigzag stitch function on your sewing machine.

As a last resort use pinking shears, but increase the seam allowances by 5mm (¼in) if you do this.

To make the tie-neck blouse

Step 1

Cut out the blouse pieces, cutting 5mm (¼in) notches as marked. On both pieces, make a small hand-stitch at point A marked on the pattern front. Place the front and back pieces right-sides together and pin them from shoulder to neck. Stitch the seam and press it open using a pressing cloth.

Point A

Step 2

Fold the tie piece in half to find the centre. Right-sides together, pin one edge of the centre of the tie to the centre of the back neck, matching the edges of the fabric. Continue pinning the tie to the neck edge of the blouse until you reach point A on each front piece. Stitch the tie in place from point A on one front to point A on the other front.

Point A   Point A

Step 3

On each front piece of the blouse, press under the front edge by 1cm (⅜in) (a), then by a further 2.5cm (1in) to create the plackets (b).

Then fold each placket back on itself, leaving the 1cm (⅜in) fold in place. Stitch across the top of each placket from point A to the outer edge. Trim the seam allowance to 5mm (¼in) (c). Turn the plackets through to the right side again, pushing the point out.

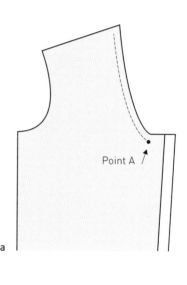

Point A

a

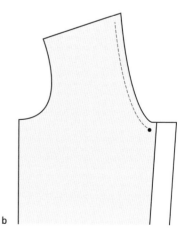

b

Step 4

Right-side in, fold the tie in half lengthways. Pin from each end to as close to point A as possible, then stitch the seam (a). Pin the safety pin inside one tie end, then use it to feed the end through until the tie is the right-side out. Turn the other tie end through in the same way (b). Press the whole tie flat, then tuck in each raw end by 1cm (⅜in) and neatly hand-stitch it closed (c).

At point A, very carefully make a snip from the edge towards – but not right up to – the point (d), so that the seam allowance at the neck can be pressed inside the tie, away from the body of the blouse. Place the tie flat and fold under the open edge of the tie so that it lies 3mm (⅛in) over the stitch line. Pin from one end of the opening to the other, then tack in place (e). Turn the blouse over and machine-stitch along the original stitch line to complete the tie (f). Remove the tacking.

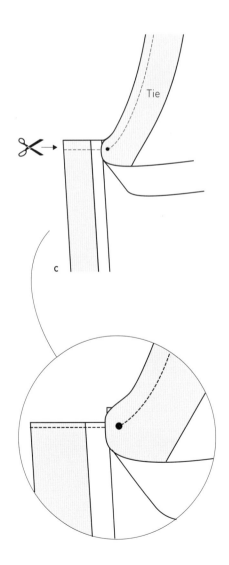

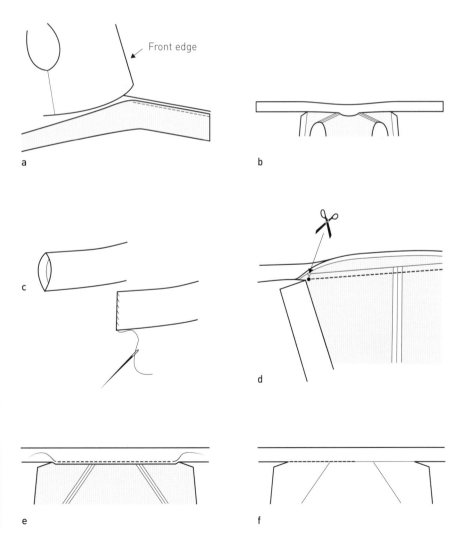

Step 5

Right-sides together, pin the sleeves to the body, matching the notches and slightly easing the fabric as necessary around the sleeve head. Stitch the seam and press the seam allowances towards the sleeve.

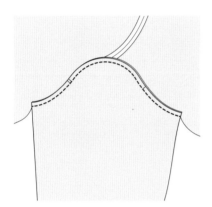

Step 6

Working from the hem to the cuff, pin the side and underarm seam on both sides. Then stitch the seams, from the hem to the cuff. Press the seam allowances open using a pressing cloth.

At this stage slip the blouse on and make any alterations needed to the sleeve length.

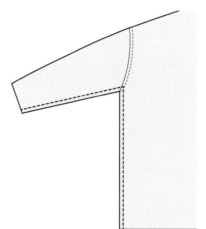

Step 7

Press each cuff over by 1cm (⅜in), then a further 3.5cm (1⅜in). Stitch the hems in place.

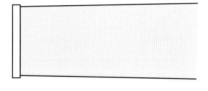

Step 8

Press the hem up by 1cm (⅜in), then a further 2cm (¾in). Open the hem out flat and at each front, fold each placket back on itself, leaving the 1cm (⅜in) fold in place (a). Stitch across each placket, along the upper pressed hem line (b). Trim each front edge corner and turn the plackets through (c).

Pin the plackets and hem in place. Stitch from one point A, down the placket, along the hem, and up the other placket to point A on the other side (d).

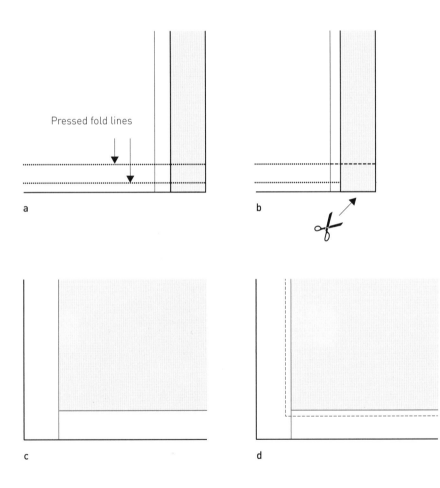

Pressed fold lines

a

b

c

d

Step 9

The first button will be placed at the top of the right placket and the rest equally spaced with the lowest one approximately 8cm (3in) up from the hem.

Using the buttonhole function on the sewing machine, test the buttonhole size on an offcut of fabric. When you are happy with the result, make the buttonholes on the blouse. Sew on buttons on the left placket to align with the buttonholes.

Press the blouse and it is ready to wear.

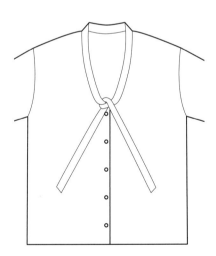

Making more of the tie-neck blouse

Print fabric

This whimsical scarf print might not look as though it would be right for this blouse, but careful placement of the pattern pieces allows the print motif to really accentuate the blouse design.

Wider, fluid ties

If you're making a blouse in a silky fabric, you might like a flouncy tie.

Step 1

Cut the tie piece 17cm (6¾in) wide. Make up the blouse following the steps on pages 72–75, but as the tie is so much wider, it is possible to stitch the ends on the wrong side, as shown. Turn the ties through, carefully pushing out the corners, and press them.

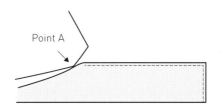

Step 2

To keep the wider tie lying smoothly around the neck, fold it over and discreetly hand-stitch the edge down around the neck line, leaving the ends in soft folds.

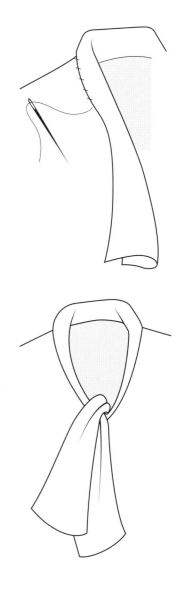

Top left and bottom right: Print fabric.
Top right and bottom left: Wider, fluid ties

Decorating the ties

There are many ways you can personalise your blouse by decorating the tie; here are a few suggestions.

Contrast colour tie
Make up the blouse using a contrast-colour fabric for the tie.

Adding trim
Stitch ribbon or braid to the centre of the outer half of the tie. You can also trim the cuffs to match.

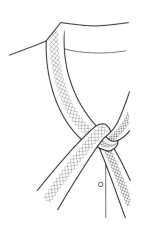

Beading the tie
Beading is a really pretty way to feminise a blouse.

If your fabric is fluid, you'll need to use some lightweight fusible interlining on the reverse of the tie before sewing on the beads.

It is easier to sew on the beads before making up the tie, but remember to only sew on beads where you want them to show – on the outer half of the neck area and the tie ends, as indicated by the shaded sections.

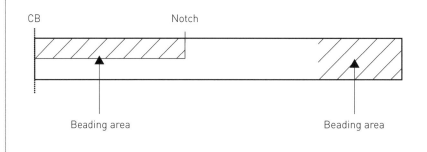

THE BOOK BAG

Developing the book bag

How you accessorise your look can define your style; think Jackie Onassis and her sunglasses, or Victoria Beckham and her Hermès Birkin bags.

I'm not sure how I would describe my style. I love the idea of the Frida Kahlo look – more is more! But it's not my style. I know accessories are as much a part of my look as are my clothes and I like to be coordinated. Whenever I'm designing or making something I'm thinking 'How am I going to wear that? What does it go with?'

I designed and made all the accessories to go with my final college collection. After college, once I was working as a designer, I went to night school to learn how to work with leather, and this gave me the skills to make simple bags and belts. Then, just before I started The Maker's Atelier, I learnt how to make traditional hand-sewn leather shoes with a bespoke leather shoemakers, Carréducker, in London.

I really enjoy making accessories, I find it just as rewarding as making clothes. When I was thinking about the key pieces that made up *The Essential Collection* this book bag was the obvious accessory to include. I use a version of this bag on most days. I have them in different colours and fabrics depending on what I'm doing and where I'm going; leather for in the city, nylon for the shops, canvas for on the beach. It is a stylish alternative to all those disposable shopping bags, and the shaped bottom of the bag means that even when you have just a few items inside, it looks good.

It's a great item to use everyday and when reproduced in a lightweight fabric like nylon cire or cotton, it can be folded up compactly and kept in your handbag – because you never know when you might have to buy something!

Here you'll find instructions for both a lined and unlined bag with two lengths of handle. It can be interpreted in patterned or plain fabric, embellished with trim or beading. It's an accessory that can reflect your own style.

Technical information

The bag

So much more stylish than a disposable shopping bag, and easy to make to complement your coat or jacket.

Sizing

Two sizes are given here, but if you keep to the same proportions you can scale up or down as you prefer.

Size	S	L
Centimetres		
Height	43	53
Width	38	46
Strap length	30	52
Strap width	2.5	3
Inches		
Height	17	21
Width	15	18
Strap length	11½	20½
Strap width	1	1¼

Fabric

Consider how heavy what you usually carry is likely to be, and choose a fabric accordingly. The unlined bag requires fabric that doesn't stretch or 'give', such as nylon cire, coated cotton, oilcloth or canvas. The lined version allows for more choice as the lining can stop your bag from 'growing'.

This item can be made in leather or suede, but choose a skin that is light enough to be sewn on your machine using a leather needle. And if you are making a bag in suede or leather, you will definitely need to line it.

The bag handles can be made from tape, as for the copper-coloured bag shown on page 82, but there are instructions for making self-fabric handles if you prefer those.

Fabric quantity

Size	S	L
Metres		
120/150cm wide	0.50	0.60
Optional lining	0.50	0.60
Tape for handles	0.80	1.20
Grosgrain for optional trim	0.80	1.00
Yards		
48/60in wide	½	½
Optional lining	½	½
Tape for handles	1	1½
Grosgrain for optional trim	1	1¼

Also required

- Fabric scissors
- Pins
- Iron and ironing board
- Sewing machine
- Sewing thread to match fabric
- Tailor's chalk
- Safety pin for turning self-fabric straps through

Sewing notes

Seam allowances are 1cm (⅜in) unless otherwise stated.

If making the unlined version, then to avoid fraying seams, if you own an overlocker or serger, overlock all the cut-out pieces before constructing the bag. Alternatively, use the overlock stitch or zigzag stitch function on your sewing machine. As a last resort use pinking shears, but increase the seam allowances by 5mm (¼in) if you do this.

Depending on the thickness of the fabric, you may need to use a heavier universal needle. For leather and suede fabrics, and some technical fabrics and finishes, use a leather needle and a longer sewing stitch: the leather needle cuts through the fabric, so the longer stitch length prevents the seam from becoming a perforated line that can tear under strain. Remember to swap a leather needle for a medium universal needle for the lining fabric.

To make the book bag

Step 1

Cut two main bag pieces, measuring 46 x 40cm (18 x 15¾in) for the small size, or 56 x 48cm (22 x 19in) for the large size.

Place the two main bag pieces right-sides together. Stitch around the two long sides and one short side.

If you are making self-fabric handles (see Step 3), then also cut two strips of fabric measuring 32 x 6cm (12½ x 2½in) for the small size or 54 x 7cm (21¼ x 2¾in) for the large size.

Step 2

At one corner, pull the front and back apart and arrange the corner point so the side seam lies directly on top of the bottom seam (a).

Draw a line across the corner, at right angles to the seam and 5cm (2in) in from the point (b).

Pin the layers together (pinning above the drawn line if pins are likely to mark the fabric), and then stitch along the drawn line, reversing at each end and taking care to keep the existing seam allowances open (c). Repeat on the other corner.

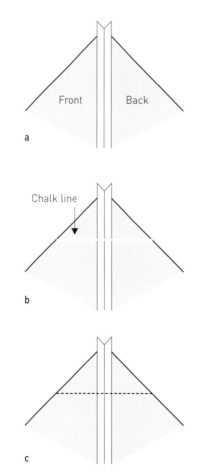

Step 3

To make self-fabric handles, fold a strip in half lengthways, right-sides in (a).

Using a 5mm (¼in) seam allowance, stitch down one long side (b).

Turn the tube right-side out using a safety pin and press it flat with the seam in the centre of one side (c).

To strengthen the strap, make two lines of stitching down the length of each strap, 3mm (⅛in) in from the edges, and one down the centre, stitching along the seam line (d). Make two straps in this way.

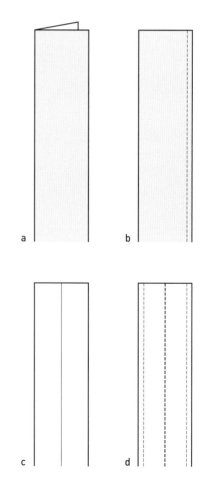

Step 4

With the bag wrong-side out, on both pieces draw a horizontal line parallel to and 3cm (1¼in) down from the top. Mark the centre point on the line with a pin or chalk mark.

On one side of the bag, pin one end of a strap 6.5cm (2⅝in) from the centre point, with the end square to the chalk line and extending 1cm (⅜in) over it. Make sure the strap isn't twisted and pin the other end in place on the other side of the pin, using the same spacing. Stitch the straps in place along the chalk line.

Step 5

Turn over the top of the bag by 1cm (⅜in), then again by a further 1cm (⅜in). Pin the hem in place and then stitch all the way around, close to the lower folded edge.

Fold the straps up over the top edge of the bag and pin them in place. Stitch all around, close to the top edge of the bag, stitching over the straps to hold them in position. If the fabric needs it, then press the bag, using a pressing cloth. Turn the bag right-side out and you're ready to shop.

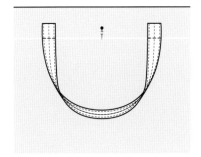

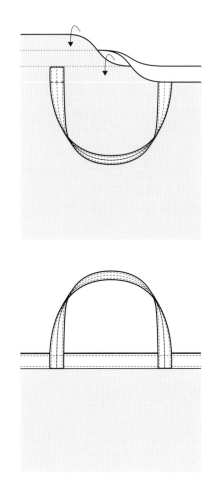

Making more of the book bag pattern

Small lined bag

Add a lining if your main fabric might stretch, or isn't very strong. Grosgrain ribbon is strong enough to make handles for a small bag.

Step 1

Cut outer bag pieces and identical pieces in lining fabric. Follow Steps 1–2 of the instructions on page 86 with both the outer bag fabric and the lining fabric.

Step 2

Turn the outer fabric bag the right-way out, but leave the lining inside out. Slip the outer bag inside the lining so that the right sides of both fabrics are together. Stitch around the top edge, leaving a 12cm (4¾in) gap in one side. Turn the whole bag right-side out through the gap, so that the right side of the outer fabric and lining are outermost, then push the outer bag inside the lining; the fabrics are not right-side out, but the whole bag is inside out with the lining on the outside. Around the top edge, roll the outer fabric 3mm (⅛in) to the inside and press the top edge. Hand-stitch the gap closed.

Main

Lining

12cm (4¾in)

Step 3

Along the top edge, mark the centre point of the bag with a pin, on both the front and back. Following Step 4 of the instructions on page 87, pin the ends of each grosgrain ribbon strap to the bag, positioning each end 5cm (2in) from the centre pin and 5mm (¼in) down from the top edge. Hand-stitch the ends of the straps to the lining only.

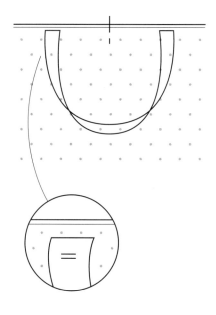

Step 4

Pin the grosgrain ribbon trim around the top edge of the bag, so that the upper edge of it is against the seam. Fold under the raw end. Stitch right around the ribbon, close to both of the edges. Fold the straps up over the top edge of the bag and stitch them in place, stitching over the existing stitches. Press the bag, using a pressing cloth, and turn it right-side out.

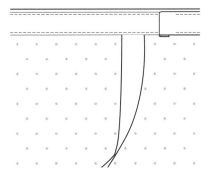

Fold-away strap

Adding this strap to your book bag lets you roll it up neatly to tuck into your handbag.

Step 1

Follow Steps 1–4 of the instructions on pages 86–87. Cut an additional piece of fabric measuring 28 x 8cm (11 x 3in), and 5cm (2in) of hook-and-loop fastening. Right-sides together, fold the fabric in half lengthways and, using a 5mm (¼in) seam allowance, stitch along the open long side and one short side. Turn the strap right-side out.

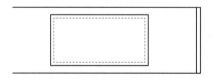

Step 2

Place the loop side of the fastening 1cm (⅜in) from the unfinished end on one side of the strap and stitch in place. Turn the strap over and place the hook side at the finished end and stitch in place.

Step 3

Place the unfinished end of the strap, with the loop fastening uppermost, 1cm (⅜in) over the chalk line on your bag, centred between the ends of a handle. Stitch it in place along the chalk line. Finish making up the bag following the instructions on pages 86–87.

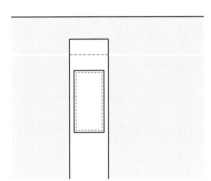

Step 4

Fold up the bag as shown.

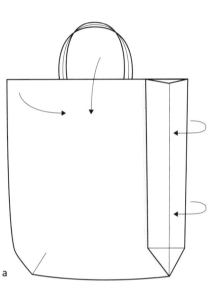

a

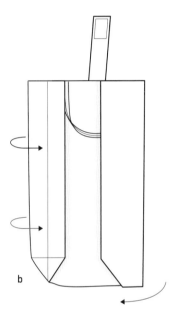

b

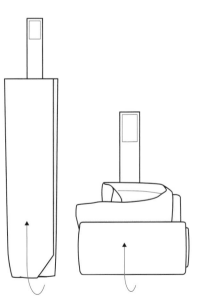

c

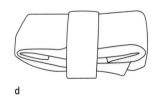

d

Leather book bag

A leather or suede bag is a very stylish accessory.

Follow the instructions for the Small Lined Bag (see page 88), using a leather needle.

To make leather handles, cut two strips of leather or suede, each measuring 34 x 2.5cm (13½ x 1in). Fold each strip in half lengthways, wrong-side in, and glue using PVA adhesive. Leave to dry. Stitch one line of stitching right down the centre of each strap and another line 5mm (¼in) to the left and right of the first line. Carefully trim off excess leather to neaten the handles.

Stitch the ends of the straps to the outside of the finished bag, placing them with the ends 10cm (4in) apart on the top edge.

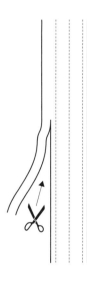

THE RAW-EDGE COAT

Developing the raw-edge coat

Several years ago I was on Brighton Beach watching the Windsurfing World Championships and I spotted one of the pro-surfers in a neoprene wetsuit coat. I'd never seen anything quite like it, but I knew I wanted one. I was living with a windsurfer at the time, so I looked at how his wetsuits were constructed and researched fabric suppliers: I soon realised that I was biting off more than I could chew. Wetsuit construction is complicated and my domestic sewing machine was not up to the task. Worse still, I do not like the smell of rubber clothing!

A couple of months later I was in Cloth House, London, and they had a roll of black coated-jersey, similar in feel to a wetsuit neoprene but without the rubber content. I bought 3 or 4 metres, as I knew I'd want to experiment and I thought it might be tricky. I had no idea how I was going to finish the edges, whether I was going to have to glue the seams, or even how my garment was going to fasten. I started experimenting: conventional seams were far too bulky so I played around with over-locked seams, but I wasn't happy with the effect. Then it dawned on me that the fabric edges weren't fraying or unravelling, so why not take a risk and leave the edges raw?

The result was the style you see here. The body of the coat is straight up and down with two patch pockets. However, the shoulder seam is angled and the sleeves are cut in two parts, curved to the shape of the arm, making the coat more comfortable to wear.

On my original coat I used buttons and buttonholes, but I found the buttonholes stretched, so here the coat has been finished with sew-on press-studs. The raw edges of my original coat proved to be more stable and have withstood years of wear and numerous machine washes.

I once read that French women buy more pieces of outerwear than women in other countries. They understand how important first impressions are, and that first impression is often made wearing a coat or jacket. That is my excuse for having made this style in numerous ways and different fabrications.

Neoprene-type or scuba fabrics are now more widely available and not limited to black, as is shown here. But I realise raw edges aren't to everyone's taste, so included in this section is a version of the coat with facings and hems, one that makes a great casual summer coat in linen or denim.

I've found that the clean lines of this style also translate well into suede or leather. The short leather jacket featured here is my idea of affordable luxury; a shop-bought jacket like this would be prohibitively expensive for me. I like the way this leather jacket transcends casual or formalwear, is light enough to wear most of the year, and thin enough to wear under an overcoat in winter.

How to wear the raw-edge coat

This coat is so versatile that it can be worn across the seasons and for all sorts of occasions. The variations mean this garment can be made in a range of fabrics, expanding its usefulness to make it a staple in any wardrobe. Here are just a few examples of how to wear it.

Top left
There's something really refreshing about a white coat. Added to that, the neoprene version (see also page 96) of the raw-edge coat has a sculptural quality to it. This creates quite a statement and can look fabulous when worn with evening or occasion-wear. Here it is styled with the embellished oversized t-shirt (see also page 140) and the satin scalloped hemmed stretch pencil skirt (see also page 28). Just add statement heels and you're ready to shine.

Top right
This is a more casual interpretation of the coat – the finished edge version made in pigment-printed washed denim (see also page 109). It's a great everyday summer coat; wear it with cotton-mix cigarette pants (see also page 48) and the over-sized t-shirt (see also page 130) for relaxed summer dressing. For cooler months this style would work well in cotton moleskin or even corduroy. One of the qualities of all cotton fabrics is how they age, becoming softer and more pliable, like a favourite pair of old jeans. A casual cotton coat like this just gets better the more it's worn.

Bottom left
Here's the neoprene coat styled in a more casual way, slipped over a pair of cigarette pants (see also page 48) and an over-sized t-shirt (see also page 130). Depending on the composition of your neoprene, your coat may even have shower-proof qualities, making it ideal for spring and autumn.

Bottom right
This is one of my standout favourites of *The Essential Collection* – the leather jacket version of the raw-edge coat (see also page 106). It's one of those garments that has great attitude, but is still so easy to wear. Shown here with the print tie-neck blouse (see also page 77) and a wrap skirt (see also page 115), it looks just as good with a t-shirt and jeans. As with the casual cotton coat, leather looks great as it ages as well as when new. The pigskin jacket I'm wearing on page 8 is about 10 years old; over time it has softened and taken on a more relaxed feel. Although there is the initial expense for the leather, it is a fraction of the cost a readymade jacket of this quality would be.

Technical information

The coat

This coat has a boxy shape, patch pockets, shallow lapels and two-part sleeves that allow a good fit.

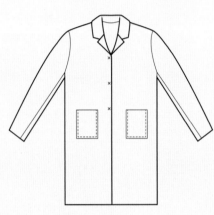

Front

Back

Sizing

Measure yourself accurately (see page 14), and check your measurements against the size chart on page 15. The chart below gives the finished sizes of the garment, so select the size that works with your measurements (remembering that garments are designed with ease to make them fit comfortably). Make notes where you differ from the given measurements and if need be, transfer the changes to your pattern pieces. For more on fitting patterns, turn to page 14.

Size	1/2	3/4	5/6	7/8
Centimetres				
Bust	110	120	130	140
Hips	110	120	130	140
Length from side neck	103	104	105	106
Overarm from side neck to cuff	74	76	78	80
Inches				
Bust	43	47	51	55
Hips	43	47	51	55
Length from side neck	40½	41	41½	42
Overarm from side neck to cuff	29	30	31	32

Fabric

This style was designed for fabrics that do not fray, especially neoprene. It also works beautifully in leather and suede, wool Melton, and felted fabrics.

Fabric quantity

Size	1/2	3/4	5/6	7/8
Metres				
120cm wide	2.20	2.20	2.50	2.50
150cm wide	1.70	1.70	2.00	2.00
Yards				
48in wide	2½	2½	2¾	2¾
60in wide	2	2	2¼	2¼

Cutting guide

Layout suggestion for 120-cm (48-in) wide fabric. The fabric is a single layer.

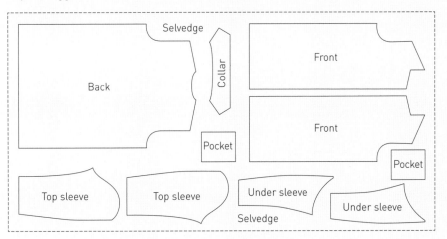

Layout suggestion for 150-cm (60-in) wide fabric. The fabric is folded in half.

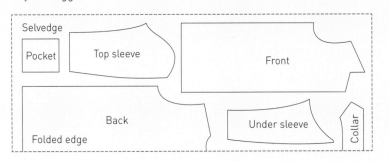

Also required

- Fabric scissors
- Pins
- Sewing machine
- Sewing thread to match fabric
- Hand-sewing needle
- 5 x 15mm (⅝in) sew-on press-stud fasteners

Sewing notes

Seam allowances are 1cm (⅜in) unless otherwise stated.

Neoprene and leather can be daunting to work with, so please refer to the fabric section (see pages 12–13) for tips on how to sew these successfully. Perfect your sewing techniques by practising stitch lengths and cutting abilities on the fabric offcuts before making your garment – this will relax you and give you confidence to enjoy the project.

The instructions given here are for exposed seams, as shown on the white neoprene coat.

To make the raw-edge coat

Step 1

Note that the paper pattern pieces are for the jacket-length garment. It is very easy to extend these to the coat length; for a finished garment length of 104cm (41in) from the side neck, simply extend the bottom edge of the front and back pieces by 44cm (17¼in).

As this design suits thicker, less pliable fabrics, place the pattern pieces on a single layer of fabric to get a clean and accurate edge to each fabric piece. Draw around each shape and then mirror each piece, making sure that the back is cut as one.

Cut out the coat pieces, cutting 5mm (¼in) notches as marked. Make a small hand-stitch at the pocket points marked on the pattern front.

Step 2

Right-sides up, place one pocket piece on each coat front, matching the top corners of the pocket with the marked pocket points. Pin and then stitch the pockets in place, taking only 3mm (⅛in) seam allowances.

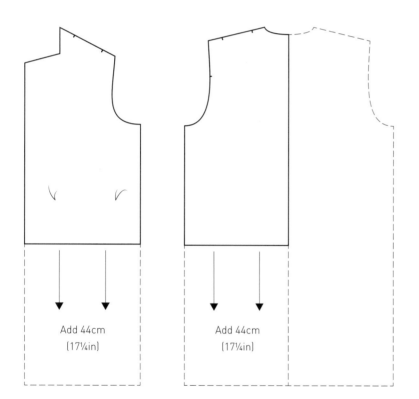

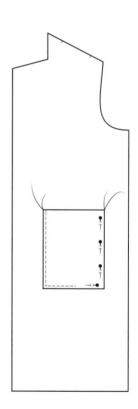

Step 3

Wrong-sides together, place the coat fronts on the back piece. Pin and then stitch the shoulder seams. Very carefully and neatly, trim the seam allowances to 3mm (⅛in).

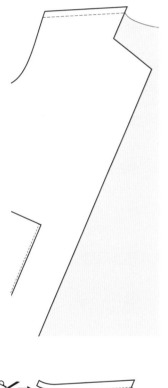

Step 4

The back neck seam is going to be under the collar so that it doesn't rub against your skin. Fold the back neck in half to find the centre back point, and mark it with a pin (a).

With the right side of the collar against the wrong side of the coat, match the collar notch to the pin at centre back and pin the collar in place (b).

Make sure that the lapel edge is equidistant from the edge of the collar on each front piece (c).

Stitch the collar in place, then carefully trim the seam allowance by starting at the lapel point and graduating to 3mm (⅛in) at the neck seam (d).

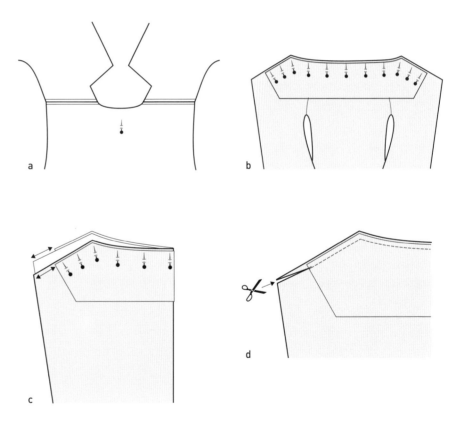

Step 5

Right-side out, pin the garment's side seams. Stitch them and then trim the seam allowances to 3mm (⅛in), as before.

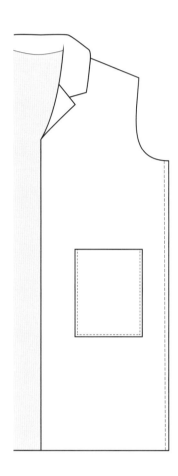

Step 6

Place the wrong sides of the sleeve pieces together, matching the notches. Pin and then stitch the seams. Trim the seam allowances to 3mm (⅛in), as before.

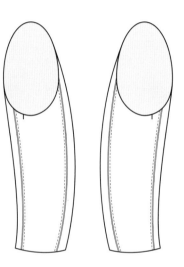

Step 7

The sleeve has a notch on the lower part of the curve, and this will line up with the side seam. The sleeve seam that is nearest the sleeve head will be at the back of the coat. Place the sleeves next to the body of the coat to make sure you insert the correct one into each armhole (a).

Turn the sleeves inside out and place one inside each of the coat's armholes. Match the sleeve notch to the side seam and the back coat notch to the higher sleeve seam (b).

Pin the sleeves in place, and then carefully stitch them. Pull the sleeves through to the right side, check that the position of each sleeve is the same, and then trim the seam allowances to 3mm (⅛in) (c).

(Illustrations opposite.)

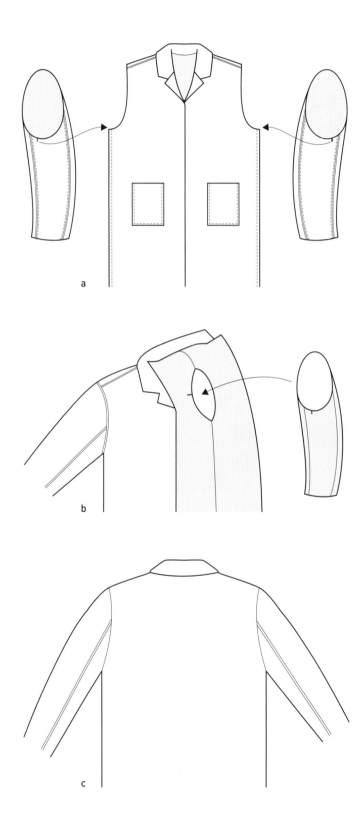

a

b

c

Step 8

Put on the coat and find the natural front cross over point for you – usually just above the fullest part of the bust. Mark this point with a pin.

Take the coat off and then mark the next four points for the press-stud fasteners, spacing them equally with the lowest one near the bottom of a pocket.

Stitch on one half of each fastener to the underside of the front edge of the right-hand coat front. Stitch the other half of each fastener to the right side of the left coat front. You can, if you wish, make a feature of any visible stitching.

If you think the coat needs a press, do this on the wrong side of the neoprene and use a pressing cloth. The coat is now ready to wear.

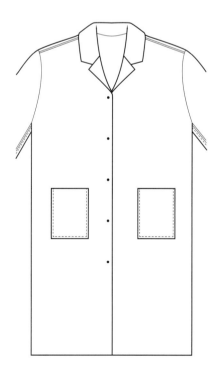

Making more of the raw-edge coat

Short leather jacket

This pattern looks great as a simple leather or suede jacket. It can be made with exposed seams in the same way as the main coat, but these instructions are for conventional seams.

Take the pattern pieces with you when you go to buy the skins; this will ensure you have exactly the right quantity and you can match the skins for quality. For other tips on working with leather, please read the fabric section (see page 13) before starting this project.

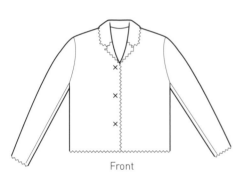

Front

Back

Step 1

You will need to cut an additional collar and two lapel facing pieces, but not the pockets. Place the pattern pieces on the skins and draw around them with tailor's chalk; use a ruler for the straight edges. Remember to mirror each pattern piece, and to cut the back as one piece.

20cm (8in)

Step 2

Glue the two collar pieces together. Spread a thin layer of PVA glue over the wrong side of one collar piece, then place the two pieces wrong-sides together, making sure there are no air bubbles. Lay the glued piece flat and weigh it down (large books are useful for this), and leave it to dry overnight.

Step 3

Place the front and back pieces right-sides together and pin them from shoulder to neck. Stitch the seams. Trim the seam allowances, or if you prefer not to do that, you can carefully glue them flat. Whichever method you use, do the same for each seam allowance other than those of the collar seam.

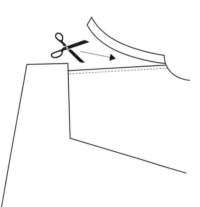

Step 4

Follow Step 4 on page 103 to attach the collar to the jacket body.

Step 5

Lay the jacket on a flat surface, with the wrong side of the jacket fronts uppermost and the collar flat.

Place the facings over the lapels and with your thumbnail, imprint the seam through the facing (b).

Trim away the facing from the edge of the collar and just above the seam imprint – leaving 5mm (¼in) to cover the seam. Use pinking shears if you are pinking the final garment edge (c), if not use sharp straight scissors to do this. Glue the facings to the jacket lapels, then weigh them down and leave to dry as before.

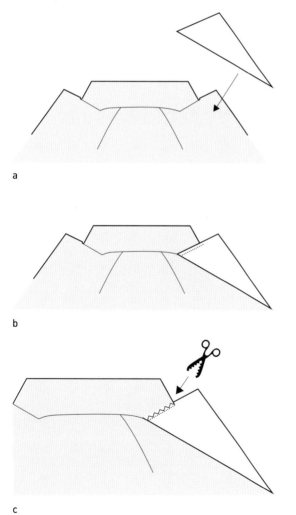

a

b

c

Step 6

Right-sides facing, stitch the side seams. Follow Steps 6–7 on pages 104–105 to make up and insert the sleeves, but do this with the pieces right-sides together so that the seam allowances are on the inside.

Step 7

If you are pinking the edges of the jacket, first place it flat on a hard surface, Carefully pink the raw edges, staying as close to the edge as you can, until you get to the top of the collar lapel. At the top of the lapel, trim in line with the existing pinked edge that covers the collar seam. Try to keep the zigzag pattern continuous along each edge.

If you prefer a straight edge, you will only need to trim the top of the lapel.

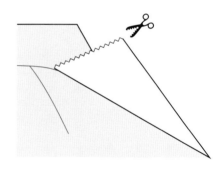

Step 8

Follow Step 8 on pages 105 to attach three 15mm (⅝in) sew-on press-stud fasteners. The jacket photographed has three 15mm (⅝in) sew-on press-studs, but you can choose alternative fastenings if you wish.

Coat with finished edges

This simple shape can easily be translated into an unlined coat with facings and hemmed edges. This opens up the choice of fabric to all sorts of woven constructions, including the pigment-printed denim version shown on page 111.

To avoid fraying seams, if you own an overlocker or serger, overlock all the cut-out garment pieces before constructing the coat. Alternatively, use the overlock stitch or zigzag stitch function on your sewing machine. As a last resort use pinking shears, but increase the seam allowances by 5mm (¼in) if you do this.

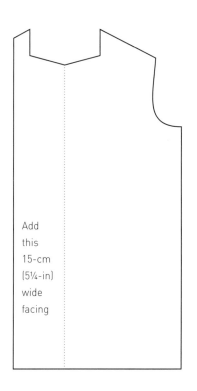

Fabric quantity

Size	1/2	3/4	5/6	7/8
Metres				
120cm wide	3.20	3.20	3.20	3.20
150cm wide	3.00	3.00	3.00	3.00
Fusible interfacing	1.10	1.10	1.10	1.10
Yards				
48in wide	3½	3½	3½	3½
60in wide	3¼	3¼	3¼	3¼
Fusible interfacing	1½	1½	1½	1½

Step 1

For this variation you need to add 3cm (1¼in) length to the hem, cuffs and tops of the pockets, and an additional 1cm (⅜in) to the other three pocket edges.

The front pieces are extended to add a facing that is cut as one with the front. Lay the front pattern piece on the fabric and chalk around it. Then mirror the pattern piece and draw the facing; this extends 15cm (5¼in) from the edge of the front to a parallel straight line, as shown. Cut two pieces of fusible interfacing to match the front facings and iron them onto the wrong side of the fabric.

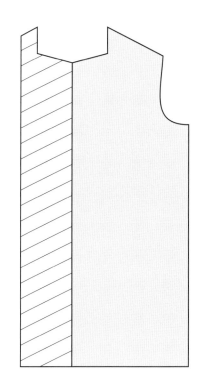

Step 2

Cut one collar piece; this is the paper collar pattern mirrored. Cut interfacing for one half of the collar and iron it onto the wrong side of the fabric.

As the seams on this garment are not exposed, remember to stitch seams with the right sides of the fabric together.

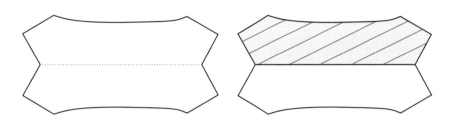

Step 3

Right-side in, fold over the top edge of each pocket piece by 3cm (1¼in). Stitch down either side of the folded section, then turn it right-side out, pushing out the corners carefully. Press under 1cm (⅜in) on the remaining three sides. Stitch across the bottom of the folded section.

Follow Step 2 on page 102 to stitch the pockets to the coat fronts.

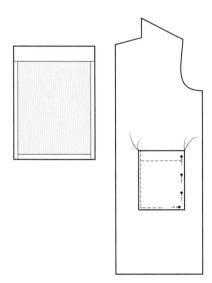

Step 4

Right-side in, fold the collar lengthways. Pin and stitch along both collar edges, taking 5mm (¼in) seam allowances (a). Turn the collar right-side out, gently pushing out the points.

With the interfaced half of the collar against the right side of the coat back, line up the centre back of the collar and the coat back. Working inside the collar, pin one edge in place, checking that the collar is equally spaced against the front facing on both sides. Stitch the seam, taking a 5mm (¼in) seam allowance (b).

Right-side in, fold the facing over on each front. Pin all the layers together – including both collar layers – from the front edge to the shoulder seam. Stitch the seams, taking 5mm (¼in) seam allowances. Make tiny snips along the curve to allow the collar and facing to sit properly (c).

Turn the facing right-side out, gently pushing out the lapel points. Press both facings using a pressing cloth.

Tack the facings in place at the shoulder seams (d).

On the right side, stitch them in place along the seam lines (e). Remove the tacking stitches.

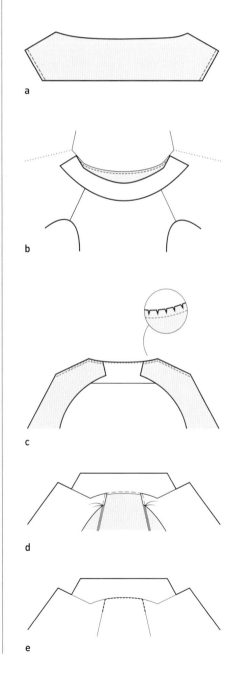

Step 5

Turn under the hem and cuffs by 3cm (1¼in) and press them.

Unfold the hem and at the front edge, turn the facing back on itself. Stitch along the pressed hem line, then trim the corner off each facing, as shown. Turn facings right-side out and gently push out the corners. Stitch the hem and cuffs in place. Each facing can be held in place by tacking it to the front, then stitching it in place along one side of the pocket, going over the line of stitching that attaches the pocket.

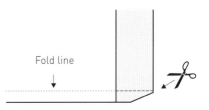

Fold line

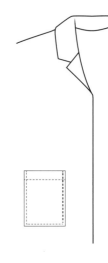

Step 6

This sample has been finished with buttons and buttonholes; follow Step 8 on pages 105 to position these.

THE WRAP SKIRT

Developing the wrap skirt

Throughout my childhood, a version of the kilt was always part of my school uniform. When I was very young, the back of the skirt's waistband was elasticated so the skirt could just be pulled on. The front had a fixed under-flap and a top flap that folded over and fastened in place with a leather strap and buckle, imitating a traditional kilt. As I progressed through to junior then on to senior school, this skirt eventually morphed into a proper kilt with a knife-pleated back and two separate over-lapping front flaps buckled in place and finished with a kilt pin.

From that first faux kilt I remember thinking that this idea of wrapping and fixing cloth was very interesting.

When I started at college, one of the final-year weave students was selling lengths of her textiles that she'd hand-woven on a dobby loom. Somehow I got the money together to acquire a length of her fabulous fabric. It was a very subtle check design in silk and linen, woven in neutral colours and finished with a fringed edge – just like a kilt. There was not enough fabric to pleat the back, but I wanted to keep this piece of fabric intact; I certainly couldn't cut it. So to shape the waist, I devised a series of dart-like folds around the back, held in place by one long length of cotton webbing tape, which I then wrapped around my hips and tied at the side.

Over the years I have persisted with this idea of wrapping and fixing cloth to create a series of garments. For example, for beach holidays I have a couple of sarong-type wraps that I have developed with tape ties. I wear these over my swimming costume as a simple cover-up.

More recently I have been playing with asymmetric hems, inspired by some of the architectural styles coming through on the catwalks. I thought I could return to the simple, one-piece-of-fabric-wrapping-around-the-body idea. However, the folds required to shape the fabric to the body negate the clean style I like to wear. So my latest version of a wrap skirt, which I have included in this collection, is actually constructed from three individually shaped pieces of fabric. When stitched together these create the illusion of a simple wrap skirt.

In its most basic form this wrap skirt is an unlined, casual summer skirt that suits a rigid, non-stretch canvas or denim fabric. The cut is designed for the skirt to sit on the lower waist, with the right-hand front overlapping to the left-hand side. The skirt is simply fastened with two over-sized press-stud fasteners; these could be replaced with a strap and buckle and or kilt pin, but I like the clean look the hidden fastenings give.

In this chapter you will find two other variations of the skirt pattern. The first is for a lined version in lightweight woollen fabric, creating a slightly more formal, trans-seasonal skirt. The second accentuates the asymmetric design with a contrast-colour panel trimming the front skirt flap. This could easily translate into a patterned skirt with coordinated trim.

How to wear the wrap skirt

As with all of the garments in *The Essential Collection*, the wrap skirt can be made in a wide variety of fabrics. Your choice of fabric will affect the way you wear your skirt. Here are a few ideas to inspire you.

Top left
This is the simplest form of wrap skirt in a pigment-dyed canvas (see also page 115), similar to 14oz denim – think of sturdy, men's denim jeans before they are first washed. This fabric gives a good 'body' to the skirt, so the wrap remains flat and neat. Here it's worn with the tie-front blouse (see also page 78) for a fresh workwear look, but if teamed with the drape-front top (see also page 30), the look would soften. Alternatively, teamed with a t-shirt it becomes a really casual item, great for summer holidays. Either way, wear this skirt with sandals for summer and ballet flats or boots for winter.

Top right
Here the skirt is made in a medium-weight linen fabric with an additional contrast cotton trim to accentuate the wrap (see also page 127). Trimming the front flap of the wrap skirt can also give this edge some body and rigidity when working with lighter-weight fabrics. This more relaxed casualwear version lends itself to being worn with the long-sleeved over-sized T-shirt in viscose jersey (see also page 130). Complete your outfit with a great pair of brogues.

Bottom left
This is the same wrap skirt as above, but styled to create a totally different end result. The skirt is worn here with the over-sized t-shirt (see also page 139) in a slinky poly/viscose jersey. The contrast between the rigid, dry handle of the canvas skirt and the soft, shiny fluidity of the jersey top adds another dimension. Accessorise with a heeled pump and the overall effect is relaxed, assured and glamorous.

Bottom right
By lining the wrap skirt, it automatically becomes a less casual garment (see also page 124). Take that a step further and use a fine checked wool and you create a very smart look indeed. This skirt coordinates beautifully with other refined fabrics, such as the fine silk of this tie-neck blouse worn here (see also page 77). The bold print works well with the fine check because the skirt's individual thread colours match the colours in the print, and from a distance the colours of the skirt meld together to create a tonal hue that coordinates perfectly. Just add a great pair of shoes and look the business.

Technical information

The skirt

This skirt creates a clean simple silhouette that flatters a wide range of body sizes and shapes.

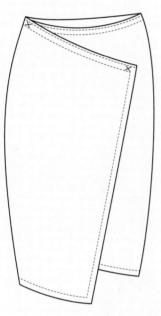

Front

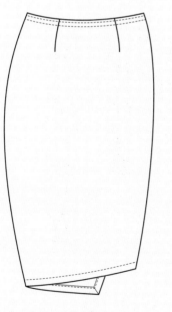

Back

Sizing

This skirt is quite fitted, so measure yourself accurately (see page 14), being sure to measure slightly below your natural waistline, as that is where the skirt sits. Check your measurements against the size chart on page 15. The chart below gives the finished sizes of the garment, so select the size that works with your measurements (remembering that garments are designed with ease to make them fit comfortably). Make notes where you differ from the given measurements and if need be, transfer the changes to your pattern pieces. Also check the lengths given on the size chart and if necessary shorten or lengthen pattern pieces at the point marked on the pattern pieces. For more on fitting patterns, turn to page 14.

Size	1	2	3	4	5	6	7	8
Centimetres								
Dropped waist	68	73	78	83	88	93	98	103
Hips	89	94	99	104	109	114	119	124
Length at CB	66	66	66	66	66	66	66	66
RH point from waist	72	72	72	72	72	72	72	72
Inches								
Waist	26½	28½	30½	32½	34½	36½	38½	40½
Hips	35	37	39	41	43	45	47	49
Length at CB	26	26	26	26	26	26	26	28
RH point from waist	28½	28½	28½	28½	28½	28½	28½	28½

Fabric

The unlined version of this skirt suits medium-weight, rigid, woven fabrics; cotton canvas or linen are ideal.

Fabric quantity

Size	1/2	3/4	5/6	7/8
Metres				
120/150cm wide	1.50	1.50	1.50	1.50
Yards				
48/60in wide	1¾	1¾	1¾	1¾

Sewing notes

Seam allowances are 1cm (⅜in) unless otherwise stated.

To avoid fraying seams, if you own an overlocker or serger, overlock all the cut-out garment pieces before constructing the skirt. Alternatively, use the overlock stitch or zigzag stitch function on your sewing machine. As a last resort use pinking shears, but increase the seam allowances by 5mm (¼in) if you do this.

Cutting guide

Layout suggestion for 120/150-cm (48/60-in) wide fabric. The fabric is a single layer.

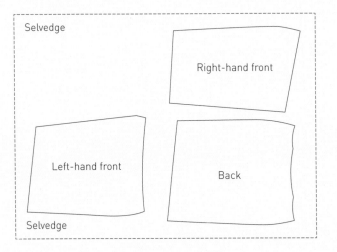

Selvedge

Right-hand front

Left-hand front

Back

Selvedge

Also required

- Fabric scissors
- Pins
- Iron and ironing board
- Sewing machine
- Sewing thread to match fabric
- 1.5m (1½yd) of 24-mm (1-in) wide herringbone tape
- Hand-sewing needle
- Two 15mm (⅝in) press-stud fasteners

To make the wrap skirt

Step 1

Cut out the trouser pieces, cutting 5mm (¼in) notches as marked. Make a small hand-stitch at the point of each dart on the back piece and at the points marked L1, L2, R1 and R2 on the pattern pieces.

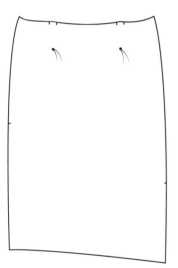

Step 2

Right-side in, fold the back piece so that the two notches of one meet and the fold line goes down to the dart point marked by the hand-stitch. Pin in place, then machine-stitch a straight line down from the notch to the point, making sure you stitch just beyond the point. Leave long thread ends at the point that you can knot to make sure the dart stitching is secure. Fold and sew the other dart in the same way. Press the darts towards the centre back.

Step 3

Right-sides together, lay the left front piece on top of the back piece, matching the side seam. Pin and then stitch the seam, then press the seam allowances open. Stitch the right front piece to the other side of the back piece in the same way.

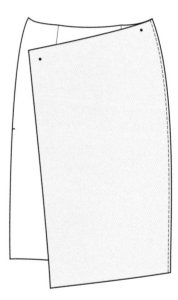

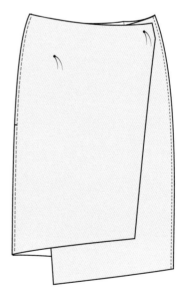

Step 4

The corners of the bottom front edges of the skirt will be mitred. To make these neat corners, turn over and press a 1cm (⅜in) hem along the two side edges and then the bottom edge. Then turn over and press another 1cm (⅜in) hem along each edge (a).

At one corner, unfold the second pressed hem (b).

Fold the corner over to meet the pressed lines, as shown (c). Press the corner crease.

Unfold the corner and then, right-side in, fold the fabric in half through the point, so that the pressed corner crease line matches on each edge (d).

Stitch along the crease line, reversing at each end. Carefully trim off the corner, 1cm (⅜in) above the line of stitching (e). Mitre the other corner in the same way.

Turn the corners through, letting the fabric naturally fall along the pressed second fold (f).

Pin the hem all the way around the three edges of the skirt, then stitch in place, stitching 3mm (⅛in) in from the edge (g).

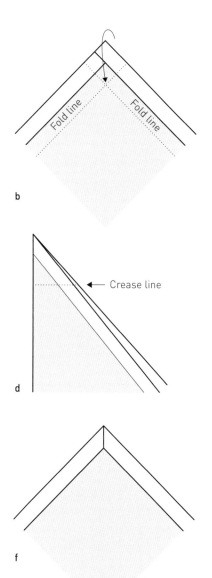

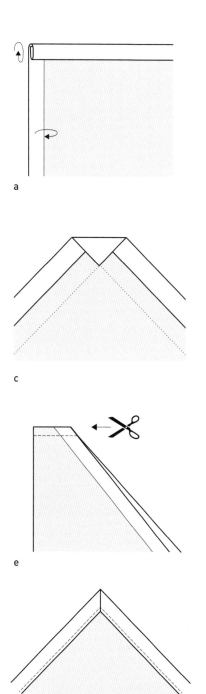

Step 5

Fold over the top edge of the skirt by 1cm (⅜in) and press in place. Pin the herringbone tape in place along the skirt's top edge, pinning the top edge just below the folded edge of the fabric. Cut the tape to length and turn under the ends to neaten them. Stitch along at the top and bottom edges and both folded ends of the tape.

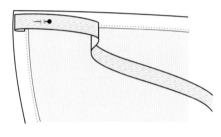

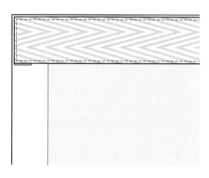

Step 6

The marked points L1, L2, R1 and R2 (see Step 1) will act as a guide for the placement of your press-stud fasteners, though some adjustment may be required to get a perfect fit. Wrap the skirt around your body, arranging it to sit comfortably just below your natural waistline. Point R1 needs to sit over point L1, so if necessary, adjust point R1 along the top edge of the skirt to achieve this.

Sew one press-stud fastener to these points, with the flat half sewn to L1 and the protruding half to R1. Then sew the protruding half of the other fastener to R2. Snap the L1/R1 press-stud fastener closed and lay the skirt flat on a table. Rub some tailor's chalk over the protruding part of the R2 fastener, and then wrap the right-hand skirt front over the left one, pressing the R2 fastener against the fabric as close to the marked L2 point as possible while still keeping the fabric lying flat and smooth. The chalk will mark the fabric and that is where you sew on the flat part of the second press-stud.

Press the skirt and it is ready to wear.

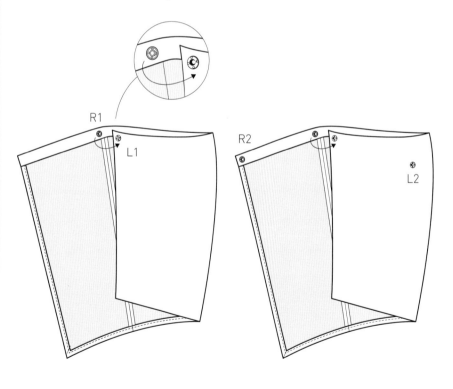

Making more of the wrap skirt pattern

Lined wrap skirt

This is an ideal solution for lighter weight fabrics, and fabrics that are likely to 'seat'.

Step 1
Cut out the main fabric following the pattern pieces. Cut the lining pieces for the back and the left-hand front 3cm (1¼in) shorter than the main fabric pieces. Cut the right-hand front piece 3cm (1¼in) shorter and 1cm (⅜in) narrower on the straight edge, as shown.

If the main fabric is lightweight, you can stiffen the right-hand skirt front with lightweight fusible interfacing.

Follow Steps 1–3 on page 120 to stitch together the main fabric pieces. Repeat the process to stitch together the lining pieces.

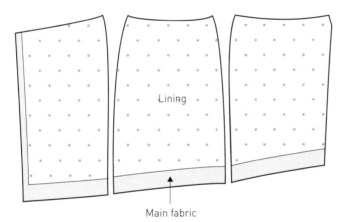

Lining

Main fabric

Step 2
Right-sides together, lay the lining over the main fabric and pin the layers together down the right-hand and left-hand straight edges. Stitch the seams, then turn the skirt right-side out. Smooth the layers so that they are both lying flat with the seam right on the edge of the left-hand front, and with 1cm (⅜in) of the main fabric folded over to the wrong side on the right-hand front. Press the skirt using a pressing cloth.

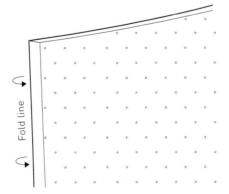

Fold line

Step 3
Turn the skirt wrong-side out again. Matching the top edge of the lining and main fabric, and making sure that the turn-under of the right-hand front stays in place, stitch right along the top edge.

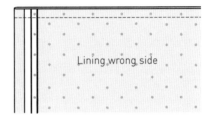

Lining wrong side

Step 4
Pin the herringbone tape to the seam allowance along the top edge, with the lower edge of the tape up against the line of stitching. Stitch the tape in place along the lower edge. Turn the skirt right-side out and press it using a pressing cloth.

Press the bottom edge of the lining up by 2cm (¾in) and the bottom edge of the main fabric by 3.5cm (1⅜in). Hand-stitch the lining to the main fabric, making sure that the lining is not pulling on the skirt in any way.

Asymmetric colour

Highlight the wrap skirt's asymmetric look with a band of complementary or toning colour along the front edge.

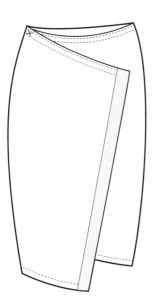

Step 1

Cut a strip of contrast fabric the length of the edge of the right-hand front, by the width you require plus 2cm (¾in) for the hems. Depending on the weight of the fabric, you can either sew the strip in place and press it flat over the main fabric, or trim off some of the main fabric underneath the strip. Unless the strip is very lightweight, you will need to trim off at least 2cm (¾in) of the main fabric, or the hems will be very bulky.

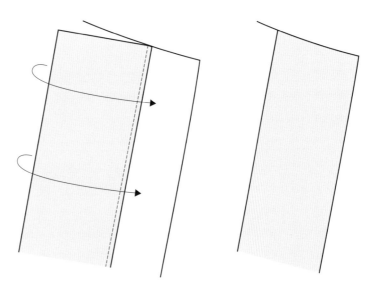

Mixing fabrics

It may sound obvious, but it's worth repeating that if you are going to stitch two different fabrics together, you need to check that they are compatible when it comes to laundering them. Choosing one fabric that is dry-clean only and another that should be washed will cause problems.

Also, it's usually best to choose fabrics of a similar weight. If they are very different then the seams can be difficult to stitch neatly and the drape of the finished garment can be affected.

THE OVER-SIZED T-SHIRT

Developing the over-sized t-shirt

The t-shirt is such a classic garment that *The Essential Collection* would not be complete without one.

The first t-shirt evolved from the all-in-one combination undergarments worn by both men and women in the 19th century. The top half of the combinations started to be worn as a separate item and became known as a t-shirt, referring to its simple T shape.

Made from a continuous circular-knitted cotton jersey fabric, the t-shirt was and is inexpensive to manufacture, easy to fit and easy to clean. The absorbent qualities of the cotton jersey fabric made the t-shirt especially popular with men working in hot environments, such as miners and stevedores. By 1913, the t-shirt became standard issue in the US Navy to be worn under the uniform, keeping the jacket fresh. And by the end of the 1920s, the t-shirt was popular as light-weight, practical outerwear.

The t-shirt's progression from a piece of functional clothing to a symbol of youth and rebellion was fuelled by Marlon Brando in *A Street Car Named Desire* and James Dean in *Rebel Without A Cause*, films released during the 1950s. Since then the basic white t-shirt has been printed, dyed, embellished and appliquéd; it is the perfect backdrop for messages of protest or allegiance.

In the early1980s, Katharine Hamnett launched her range of over-sized white t-shirts with large, black, block-letter slogans, including her anti-drug message CHOOSE LIFE; a message later appropriated by the pro-life anti-abortion movement.

But the graphic t-shirt is most synonymous with the music industry. From the 1960s onwards, rock bands have produced their own graphic t-shirts to merchandise on tours. Some of these t-shirts now sell for large amounts at auction – a vintage 1966 Beatles *Butcher Cover* album t-shirt sold for US$20,000.

More recently the luxury designer brands have produced their own versions of the classic t-shirt, with labels like Gucci commanding prices in excess of $1,500. But the majority of t-shirts are still very affordable, so why do I make my own?

Well, I can never find a fit I'm truly happy with. Most women's t-shirts are too fitted, and men's have too tight a crew neckline. Then there is the fabric quality: I prefer jersey fabrics with some elastane content, not for the fit but for the weight; it gives the T-shirt drape so that it hangs well on the body.

Of course there are limitations to creating my own t-shirts. Even If I can find coordinating rib fabric to trim the neckline, I find this incredibly tricky to do with an ordinary domestic machine. So the style I have evolved is a simple scoop neck that sits just below my collarbones. The neck, cuffs and hem are finished with a twin-needle stitch line that gives a professional finish. This pared-back style can be made in plains, stripes and prints, it can be embellished in many different ways, and can be created in a length to suit you.

How to wear the over-sized t-shirt

The over-sized t-shirt is just such a versatile garment; most of us must have at least one in our wardrobes and our own ways of wearing it. But here are some suggestions for how to wear the different versions you can make from this pattern, from super-relaxed to uber-glam!

Top left

The long-line t-shirt (see also page 139) is the perfect partner to wear with leggings or skinny jeans. Make it to the length that suits your body shape and makes the most of your legs; it's such a comfortable combo that hides a multitude of sins. But when it's reworked in slinky jersey with a striking print as shown here, it's anything but slouchy. Accessorise with a statement necklace, a fabulous pair of shoes and a great little bag like the leather book bag (see also page 92) and you're ready to go.

Top right

Alternatively, just choose to be far more relaxed and pair the basic over-sized t-shirt (see also page 130) with the cigarette pants. Here the t-shirt is in a narrow-striped cotton-mix jersey worn with the fine herringbone weave cotton-stretch pants (see also page 48). I like to wear a darker colour on my bottom half, especially with slim-line trousers; I think it's more flattering.

Bottom left

The long-sleeved t-shirt (see also page 139), with its deeper hem and cuffs, makers a great alternative to heavy-weight knits. It works well with all sorts of skirt and trouser styles; here it's worn with The Wide-legged Trouser from The Maker's Atelier pattern range (see also page 142). The trick with wearing baggy on baggy like this is to keep your fabrics fluid with plenty of drape. Also carefully consider the length of the top; too long and you'll just look drowned, and too short and the proportions will be wrong. Add a necklace or wrap around a scarf to pull your look together.

Bottom right

An embellished t-shirt (see also page 140) can go two ways – frumpy or really cool. I prefer the latter and my way of achieving this is not to be too precious. Try rolling the sleeves to give it a nonchalant air, and then layer on the bling with the metallic stretch skirt (see also page 18) and kitten-heeled sling-backs. Of course, you can take it further and add in the ankle socks, but for some that might be a step too far. With so much going on, keep your jewellery to a minimum; go for earrings or bangles but not both – you really want to avoid the Christmas tree look!

Technical information

The t-shirt

This easy-fit t-shirt has an over-sized body while fitting flatteringly at the shoulders and neck.

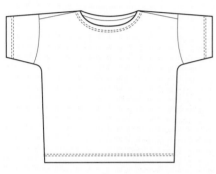

Front

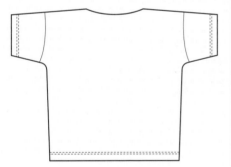

Back

Sizing

Measure yourself accurately (see page 14), and check your measurements against the size chart on page 15. The chart below gives the finished sizes of the garment, so select the size that works with your measurements (remembering that garments are designed with ease to make them fit comfortably). Make notes where you differ from the given measurements and if need be, transfer the changes to your pattern pieces. For more on fitting patterns, turn to page 14.

Size	1/2	3/4	5/6	7/8
Centimetres				
Bust	106	116	126	136
Hips	98	108	118	128
Length from side neck	65	66	67	68
Overarm from side neck to sleeve edge	46	48	50	52
Inches				
Bust	41½	45½	49½	53½
Hips	38½	42½	46½	50½
Length from side neck	25½	26	26½	27
Overarm from side neck to sleeve edge	18	19	20	21

Fabric

This t-shirt suits light- to medium-weight, single jersey fabrics in cotton and other fibres. The inclusion of elastane isn't essential, but you may prefer the handle these fibres give. If you are new to working with stretch fabrics, try a medium-weight, pure cotton, single jersey and use a zigzag stitch

Fabric quantity

Size	1/2	3/4	5/6	7/8
Metres				
120cm wide	2.00	2.00	2.00	2.00
150cm wide	1.80	1.80	1.80	1.80
Yards				
48in wide	2¼	2¼	2¼	2¼
60in wide	2	2	2	2

Cutting guide

Layout suggestions for 120-cm (48-in) wide fabric. The fabric is a single layer.

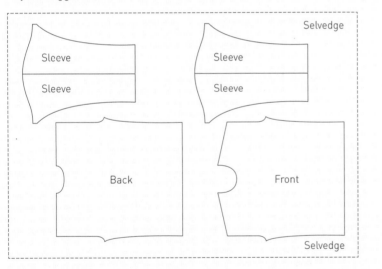

Layout suggestions for 150-cm (60-in) wide fabric. The fabric is folded in half.

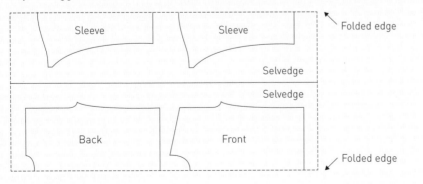

Also required

- Fabric scissors
- Pins
- Sewing machine
- Iron and ironing board
- Sewing thread to match fabric: 2 reels to allow twin-needle stitching if wanted

Sewing notes

Seam allowances are 1cm (⅜in) unless otherwise stated.

When sewing with jersey fabrics, always use a ballpoint or jersey needle. Stitch using a straight stitch, but apply a slight tension to the fabric as you feed it through; this will mean that your seam is less likely to break when the fabric stretches.

On the sample, a twin needle has been used to finish the neck, cuffs and hem, but a simple zigzag stitch can be substituted for that.

To make the over-sized t-shirt

Step 1

Cut out the t-shirt pieces, selecting the short sleeve and shallow hem and cutting 5mm (¼in) notches as marked.

Step 2

Place the front and back pieces right-sides together, matching the notches, and pin them from shoulder to neck. Stitch the seams and press the seam allowances open using a pressing cloth.

Step 3

With right-sides together, pin the sleeves to the t-shirt body, matching the notches. Stitch them in place then press the seam allowances open.

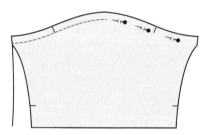

Step 4

Right-sides together and matching the notches, on each side pin from the underarm point to the cuff, then from the underarm down to the hem. Stitch both side seams, working from the hem to the cuff. Make small snips into the seam allowance at underarm point, taking care not to snip the stitching, and press the seam allowances open.

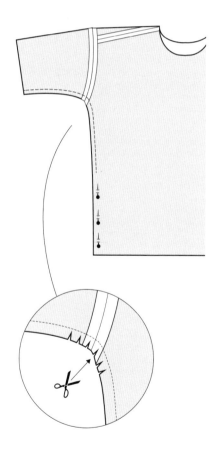

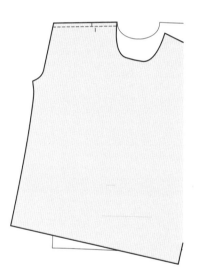

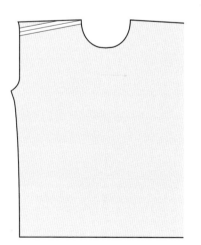

Step 5

On the wrong side, turn under the neck edge by 1cm (⅜in) and tack in place. Turn under the cuffs and hem by 2cm (¾in) and tack those in place.

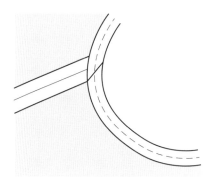

Step 6

Change to a twin needle and re-thread the sewing machine. On the right side, stitch around the neck with the twin needle set-up, taking a 5mm (¼in) seam allowance. Remove the tacking stitches.

On the right side, stitch around the cuffs and hem with the twin needle set-up, taking 1.5cm (⅝in) seam allowances. Remove the tacking stitches.

Press the t-shirt and it is ready to wear.

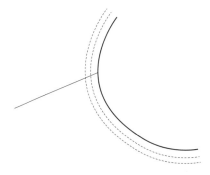

Making more of the over-sized t-shirt

Long-sleeved t-shirt

As well as long sleeves, this variation has deeper cuffs and hem.

Step 1
Select the long sleeve and deep hem t-shirt pattern pieces. Cut out and make up the t-shirt following Steps 1–5 on pages 136–137.

Step 2
On the wrong side, turn under the cuffs and hem by 8cm (3¼in) and tack in place. On the right side, stitch around each hem with the twin needle set-up, taking 7.5cm (3in) seam allowances. Remove the tacking stitches.

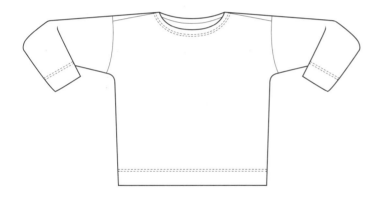

Long-line t-shirt

In this version, the body of the t-shirt has been extended to create a tunic style.

Step 1
When laying out your pattern pieces, extend the length of the front and back by 20cm (8in). Make up the t-shirt following Steps 1–6 on pages 136–137.

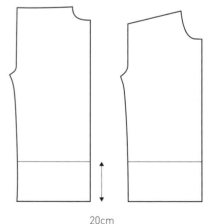

20cm
(8in)

Top left: Long-sleeved t-shirt.
Bottom right: Long-line t-shirt.

Add embellishment

A simple t-shirt really suits all sorts of embellishment, and here's just one example using plastic gemstones. It is important to select a jersey fabric that can take the weight of the embellishment chosen; for this sample a medium-weight crepe jersey was used.

Step 1

Cut out and make up the t-shirt following Steps 1–6 on pages 136–137. Add the twin needle effect at the shoulder and sleeve seams if your embellishment crosses these seams; the twin stitching flattens the seam.

Step 2

The gemstones here have been glued in place. To do this, lay the t-shirt flat on a hard surface. Slip a sheet of plain paper inside the garment, separating the front from the back in the area you want to embellish. Starting with the front, plan the layout of the stones, then carefully glue them in place using a suitable, washable adhesive (see Resources on page 142). When these have dried, turn the t-shirt over and repeat the process on the back.

Resources

Acknowledgments

The Maker's Atelier
Visit www.themakersatelier.com
to see the full range of patterns
(including The Bomber Jacket on
page 21, The Box Shirt on page 51
and The Wide-Leg Trousers on page
133) and making-kits available.
Subscribe to the newsletter, which
includes further ideas for customising
and making more of the patterns.

I shop for fabrics everywhere; these
are my favourite places.

Cloth House
www.clothhouse.com
*Great selection of fabrics including the
neoprene used for the Raw-Edge Coat.*

Ditto Fabrics
www.dittofabrics.co.uk
*Fabulous ex-designer fabrics at
affordable prices.*

MacCulloch & Wallis
www.macculloch-wallis.co.uk
*Excellent range of haberdashery; they
also stock fabric and pattern paper.*

The Vintage Workshop
www.thevintageworkshopuk.com
*Vintage fabric including lining
fabric, plus ribbons and trims.*

Til The Sun Goes Down
www.tilthesungoesdown.com
Beautiful vintage-inspired fabrics.

Walter Reginald
www.walterreginald.co.uk
Wide range of leather and suede.

Wayward
www.wayward.co
*Vintage fabric and extensive vintage
haberdashery range.*

I'd like to thank my friends who've
been around forever and given me
loads of encouragement – Kate,
Joyce, Jane, Kevin, Tristan, Nick,
Vikki and Kay. John Miles, my
exceptional tutor and reason I got
into the RCA. Fiona Shafer for her
wise words. Donal Gordon for his
sound advise and support. The
indomitable Gill Thornley at Ditto
who first suggested I publish my own
patterns. The brilliant Eighth Day
Design especially Jo, Sarah and Jon.
My fabulous models – Amelia, Clare,
Floret, Lou, Maria and Sarah.

Amelia Shepherd and Katya De
Grunwald for capturing the essence
of The Maker's Atelier. Jeni Dodson
for making everyone look good.
Vanessa Masci for the book design.

Lisa Pendreigh at Quadrille
Publishing without whom this book
would never have happened, and of
course my editor, Kate Haxell; thank
you I've really enjoyed it and I've
learnt loads.

DEDICATION
**To my family: my father who taught
me about bespoke; Stephen
for his creativity; Anne for my first
pair of fabric shears; Jill for being
The Maker's Atelier's biggest fan;
Patrick for being so well dressed;
but most of all my mum, who taught
me how to sew and gave me
my first sewing machine.**

Publishing director: Sarah Lavelle
Commissioning editor: Lisa Pendreigh
Project editor: Kate Haxell
Creative director: Helen Lewis
Designer: Vanessa Masci
Fashion photographer: Amelia Shepherd
Still life photographer: Katya De Grunwald
Illustrator: Jon Callard
Stylist: Frances Tobin
Hair and make-up artist: Jeni Dodson
Production director: Vincent Smith
Production controller: Emily Noto

First published in 2017 by Quadrille Publishing
Pentagon House, 52-54 Southwark Street,
London SE1 1UN

Quadrille Publishing is an imprint of Hardie Grant
www.hardiegrant.com.au | www.quadrille.co.uk

Cataloguing in Publication Data: a catalogue for
this book is available from the British Library.

ISBN 978-1-84949-904-0

10 9 8 7 6 5 4 3 2 1

Printed in China